The Pri...
Adventure

HAMISH MacINNES

The Price of Adventure

More mountain rescue stories
from four continents

Hodder & Stoughton
LONDON SYDNEY AUCKLAND TORONTO

I would like to thank Betsy Brantley for so patiently correcting this manuscript and for her constructive suggestions.

British Library Cataloguing in Publication Data

MacInnes, Hamish
    The price of adventure : more mountain rescue stories from four continents.
    1. Mountaineering—Accidents and injuries
    I. Title
    363.1'4   GV200.183

    ISBN 0 340 26323 7

Hodder and Stoughton Editorial Office: 47 Bedford Square, London WC1B 3DP.

To those who died on these rescues,
and to the men who tried to save them.

CONTENTS

Contents

ILLUSTRATIONS

between pages 96 and 97

The West Face of Siula Grande[1]
A painful descent[1]
Traverse from the couloir onto the Bonatti Pillar
Aiguille Verte and the Drus[2]
Members of the Chamonix rescue team[2]
Mount Kenya from the north[3]
The rescue area below Shipton's Notch[4]
Gerd Judmaier[5]
Rescue on Beinn an Dothaidh
A Sea King lands in bad weather
Beinn Achaladair
The 'spirit' map
Duncan Smith of Achallader farm
Mount Washington[6]
Hugh Herr adjusting a climbing foot[7]
A hard lead on his artificial feet[7]
White Elbe valley from Meadow Chalet[8]
North Face of Mieguszowiecki[9]
Mount Cook from the west[10]
Don Bogie brings in Phil Doole[11]
Phil Doole[12]

CREDITS

1 Joe Simpson
2 Emmanuel Schmutz
3 John Cleare/Mountain Camera
4 Dr R. Margreiter
5 Dr Oswald Oelz
6 David Stone

7 S. Peter Lewis
8 Valda Spusta
9 Dennis Gray
10 Bob Munro
11 Russell Braddock
12 Dick Price

1

TO BEGIN

This collection of true rescue stories comes from various corners of the globe. Most are told by the rescuers or the rescued themselves, sometimes by both. The majority of the contributors are known to me, and though it is common for such people to underplay the traumas and hardships which they experienced, the harsh terrain and weather are guaranteed to provide raw material for adventure of a high order. There is no need to highlight such accounts. The events speak for themselves.

Rescue procedure varies in different parts of the world. In Britain we associate the sport of mountaineering with the freedom of the hills, but in certain countries restrictions have been imposed as a result of the sheer volume of accidents. This has been met with criticism from various quarters where no such curtailment exists.

In many parts of the world there is a charge for mountain rescue, but in Britain it is on a voluntary basis, which includes the use of rescue helicopters. These are mainly operated by the RAF, whose crews are professional Search and Rescue (SAR) personnel. They also answer sea and coastguard emergencies.

The mode of rescue can vary from area to area. The crags of the English Lake District provide a prolific number of accidents, but the rescue operation is often of short duration, as many of the cliffs are close to roads. In more remote areas such as the Alps of New Zealand, the Americas, Russia and arctic regions, mountain rescue, until the advent of the helicopter, was usually a major and protracted logistical problem.

One never ceases to be amazed at the resilience of man and, more especially, woman. With a will to live, people survive seemingly impossible hardships, far beyond the design parameters of the human frame. For an example, take the case of a Dutchman, Antonias Peters, from near Alkmaar, who in August 1984 came to Scotland on a hillwalking holiday.

He was a fit man, having run twenty marathons, and on this, one of a dozen visits to the country, he was 'Munro bagging'. For Sassenachs that means climbing peaks of over 3000 feet (915 metres). He headed north and west to upper Loch Etive in Argyllshire, a wild and beautiful sanctuary with few roads, where one has only sheep, red deer and the ubiquitous midge for company.

There is also a particular attraction in roaming through natural wilderness. You can let an overtaxed mind play second fiddle to your body, or just relish the elation of being at one with nature. The Scottish Highlands can be especially restful and liberating, the colours soothing, and the air pure as the water tumbling from the hills. But a slip or a breaking handhold can change everything. In Antonias' case he fell into a precipitous streambed, badly breaking his thighbone, and lay for five days, some of this time in icy water, before he was rescued.

He was on the remote Beinn nan Aighenan, a peak overlooking Glen Kinglass, when he peered into the depths of a gully and, to get a better view, stood on a clump of heather which overhung the edge. This proved to be his literal downfall as he thudded down the face with his rucksack still on his back and landed in the bouldery bed of the stream. Crawling to the edge of the channel, he took stock of his situation. It was impossible to climb out. The walls were steep and slippery, but Ton, as he likes to be called, didn't despair. He was determined to stay there, if need be, until his leg mended sufficiently, like a wild animal.

He swallowed some painkilling Panadol tablets and regretted that he didn't have a whistle to attract attention. He had tried to buy one at various villages since he started his trek. His only consolation lay in the fact that it was highly unlikely anyone would ever hear distress signals in such a remote part of Scotland. Perhaps a dozen parties a year ventured down this side of the Beinn nan Aighenan.

Ton, then thirty-two, is a teacher of mathematics and with the tidiness of a logical mind he resolved to write up his diary and carefully ration the small supply of food which he had in his rucksack. But the next day torrential rain fell, causing a flash flood, and the channel, from which there was no escape, transformed into a constricted torrent. He was swept downstream and over several small waterfalls. Agonisingly, he managed to crawl sixteen feet, but it took him four hours. About twenty-four hours later he was carried further down, this time getting lodged by his bad leg in a submerged tree. Now he was in an even worse predicament than before. His only escape was up a twelve-foot vertical holdless rock wall.

Between his initial fall and the two flood excursions he had come down almost a thousand feet. The food which he had so carefully rationed had been lost in the floods. The remains of a flask of tea, and of course an unlimited supply of fresh water, was all he had left.

Despite his painful injury somehow or other he managed to scale the rock face in a Herculean effort. At the top he lay in agony, but when he managed to take stock of the surroundings he saw that the floor of Glen Kinglass was now visible, up which, from the shores of Loch Etive, runs a single-track private dirt road. There is a gamekeeper's cottage at the fringe of the loch and almost directly below Ton's gully lay Glen Kinglass Lodge.

He began shouting for help, for about six hours, and his cries were heard. During the stalking season Glen Kinglass Lodge, like many others in the Highlands, is let out for paying guests. On the Sunday, 5 August, the current stalking tenant had gone for a walk in the direction of the gully with a friend and was later followed by his wife. She clearly heard calls from above and when they later all met up in the lodge, she rebuked her husband for his somewhat alarming and persistent shouting. He of course denied this and was supported by his companion. They finally dismissed the subject, assuming that it must have been some hillwalker fooling about. Later they realised that the husband and his friend had been within a couple of hundred yards of the Dutchman, but they didn't hear a thing.

Ton continued to lie above the stream waving his anorak and calling for help, his daily distress routine. By the grace of God next morning Tim Healy, a gamekeeper employed by the estate, happened to hear calls from the direction of the gully. He thought at first it was a sheep but concluded the ground was too steep. Any sheep up there would be a dead one. With Tim was a stalking gillie, Alastair Loder, and so these two experienced hillmen took out their telescopes and 'spied' the steep area around the gully where the Beinn nan Aighenan stream leaps over a huge waterfall. They spotted Ton's waving anorak and set off a flare in his direction to let him know he had been spotted. Tim assumed there must be another member of the party dead in the steep gully. So he fired a second flare, which was a prearranged signal for other members of the stalking party to bring up a wheeled deer transporter, which Tim reckoned would be needed to take down the body.

From the lodge the Oban police were contacted by telephone and Sergeant Kenny Aird requested a rescue helicopter from RAF Pitreavie in Fife, the Helicopter Co-ordinating Centre. On this occasion the one closest was a Naval Sea King, based at HMS *Gannet* at Prestwick and used for anti-submarine patrols in the eastern Atlantic. This machine is fitted with a 300-foot-long winch wire and, once on the scene, a doctor and a winchman were lowered down to Ton. In minutes he was splinted and winched aboard on the helicopter stretcher and flown directly to Crosshouse Hospital in Kilmarnock where he made a satisfactory recovery. Tim Healy is convinced that, even if he hadn't spotted the Dutchman, Ton would have eventually made it down to the lodge, such was his determination to survive.

What is the future of mountain rescue? Modern technology has done much to take some of the grind out of the rescuer's burden and indeed to make his job safer. However, the frequency of call-outs has increased with the growth of both population and leisure – in some areas at an alarming rate, so that despite the greater availability and capability of helicopters, rescue man-hours have not decreased.

Though rescue dogs have still a vital role in the location of lost or buried people, the electronic avalanche bleeper has made avalanche search much safer. Only a few years ago, searching an avalanche tip or going into an avalanche-prone area was probably the greatest hazard facing a rescue team. Now, when you switch your bleeper to transmit if exposed to avalanche risk, your colleagues can home in on you should you be buried.

The greatest single advance in mountain rescue over the past twenty years has, of course, been the use of helicopters. In Britain, the Sea King and the Wessex have been the faithful Search and Rescue workhorses. The Sea King is ideally suited for long sorties over the ocean. It has a range of 930 km (577 miles) and in addition to four crew can carry up to seventeen people. The problem with the Sea King, and indeed all large helicopters, in a mountain environment is excessive downwash from the rotors, which can be positively dangerous in exposed situations. The Wessex is a smaller model with a three-man crew and can carry up to twelve passengers. Its range is 500 km (310 miles). Unfortunately, the Wessex may shortly be retired from Search and Rescue service.

In the European Alps, the French Alouette II and III are favoured for their compactness and high-altitude capability. Their sister machine, the Lama, is the mighty mouse of the helicopter stable. As well as being able to lift its own weight, it holds the world helicopter altitude record of over 41,000 feet (12,491 metres) but its cabin is too cramped to take a stretcher. Other teams use the Bell Iroquois, the Sioux, the twin-engined Bolkow and even the gargantuan Chinook with its capacity of four crew and forty-four passengers. Normally this twin-rotor helicopter is only used for transporting personnel to a search area.

It is but a matter of time before a cheap Superlite location beacon is available to the intrepid cross-country skier, climber or hillwalker. This will mean that any time of the day or night and in any weather, he or she can be located with a minimum of hassle. One must look forward to such well-meaning devices with mixed feelings however, for in this age of conformity, what independence still exists to roam the hills is very precious. Mountaineering and exploration are in danger of being tethered by a safety-conscious umbilical cord. Let's hope that in the effort to prevent adventurers being killed we don't kill the quest for adventure.

2

LUCKY JOE

Joe Simpson fell the best part of 2000 feet in the Alps in an avalanche on the North-East Face of Les Courtes. 'I didn't have any helmet on. Only my legs were buried when I finally came to rest, and apart from a cut head and bruising, I was otherwise unhurt . . . I was bloody stupid and I deserved to die.'

Joe Simpson had already had one dramatic demonstration that someone somewhere was keeping half an eye on him when climbing the Bonatti Pillar in 1984, and in 1985 he was to survive an even more spectacular climbing accident on the other side of the world on the West Face of Siula Grande in the Peruvian Andes.

But first the Bonatti Pillar.

Joe and his climbing partner, Ian Whittaker, had virtually finished the climb and managed to get to a bivouac ledge in gathering darkness and swirling cloud. Probing the corners of their lair for the night with the aid of their headlamps, they saw that it was in fact a huge pedestal which formed the right wall of a high-angled corner they had just ascended. Above the pedestal there was no continuing corner, only a vertical smooth wall. There was no way up there, so they counted themselves lucky that they had come across this providential ledge when they did.

Joe found an old piton above the ledge, which he decided to use for a belay, but this wasn't much good for protecting Ian, who was further along. Ian tied a belay rope to a rock flake which was close to him and passed the end to Joe who secured it to the peg. The rope now acted as a sort of handrail between the two of them. Joe also found an additional spike behind him and put a couple of slings over this to which he tied himself for added security, then he clipped on to the handrail and settled in for the night, the great void beneath them masked in the darkness. Joe had zizzed off when he heard Ian's voice.

'Do you think we're safe from rocks here? I was going to sleep without my helmet on.'

'Safe as houses,' Joe returned, for above them were great overhangs and any rocks falling would be well out from the face and their ledge. 'But,' he continued, hedging his bets, 'I'll keep mine on just the same.' In the light of his headlight Joe watched Ian take off his helmet and place it beside him, then clip himself on to the handrail in case he literally dozed off during the night.

As if on cue there was a frightening noise, a sort of groaning followed by a violent tug on both their safety ropes. They were falling, cocooned in their bivvy bags. Then they jerked to a halt on their handrail rope, both hanging like socks on a clothesline. The old peg and the rock spike had fortuitously held. The ledge, now disintegrated, crashed 2000 vertical feet down the face to the couloir, then bounced another thousand feet to the glacier.

Presently in the anonymous darkness all was quiet. Joe wondered about his companion, he seemed to recall a cry. Had Ian plunged to his death? But Ian's reassuring Lancastrian accent floated out of the night. He was all right and needed a drink! He had a head injury and, hanging there, Joe examined his scalp by the light of his headlamp. It wasn't too serious. They were grateful to be alive. Had the ledge collapsed only five minutes before, when they weren't belayed, they would now be mutilated messes on the Dru Glacier.

Gradually they took stock of their position and found that they had lost all their gear, even their boots. Joe in fact still had one and he now disgustedly tossed this useless item in the wake of the rock fall. Ian had even lost one of his socks and had to utilise a woollen climbing mitt in lieu.

With the beam of Joe's headlamp they saw that their climbing rope, their lifeline, was shredded by the fallen rocks and hung uselessly down the corner below them. The two young men then examined their belays with some trepidation. They saw to their consternation that the spike which Joe had put the slings over as an added safety precaution had disappeared, though the karabiners were still clipped to his harness. The slings must have parted when the ledge went. Joe next examined the old ring peg to which they were attached at his end of the now V'd handrail. He observed that it had bent and then, pulling sideways on it to get a better look, he saw to his horror that it moved. On Ian's side the case was no better. The other handrail belay, the spike, had sheared off at the bottom with the ledge but somehow still held, even though they saw splinters of rock still falling out of the gap surrounding it.

The climbers were now in an unenviable position, unable to move, with a loose peg at one end of the rope and a shaky spike on the other. They had no gear left to help safeguard themselves and any violent movement could send them both crashing down the face. Even to climb up the rope would involve too much disturbance and anyhow they were still trapped in their bivvy bags.

Joe and Ian hung on their line for twelve hours, frightening themselves when they had to move to overcome cramps. They were both forced together at the bottom of the V in the rope. It was like Russian roulette where any movement could trigger off the vibration which would dislodge the peg or loosen the flake further.

They shouted throughout the night and signalled with their headlamp to the Charpoua hut, for it was in line of sight from where they were. In the cold light of dawn the frightening drop they could now see below worked overtime on the imagination. Salvation came in the form of an Alouette III helicopter. Their distress signals had been seen. It eased its way towards the face until it hovered like a giant humming-bird not fifty feet away. The two climbers pointed at their stockinged feet, then held their arms up in a 'V' to indicate that they required help. Possibly the understatement of the year. The pilot took all this in and after giving a thumbs up he swung down towards Chamonix.

Members of the Chamonix rescue team were dropped by helicopter on a ledge above the pair and set up a hand winch. Some time later a guide came down on the steel winch wire to evacuate them. After they were both taken up to the ledge, the Alouette came in and they were picked up on a helicopter winch and lifted up into the cabin.

Joe has since speculated on his rashness in throwing away his remaining boot, for he heard a few days later that a French climber had found a climbing boot in the couloir at the bottom of the Dru and it worried him to think that this may have been the other one of the pair.

The scene changes to the Peruvian Andes in 1985. Joe's companion is twenty-two-year-old Leicestershire-bred Simon Yates, now living in Sheffield. Their objective was one of the highest unclimbed mountain walls in Peru, the 6360-metre (17,447-foot) West Face of Siula Grande. They set up their Base Camp at 4500 metres at the top of the high Quelrada Sarapoquoucha, a superbly isolated place.

After one abortive attempt on the wall, driven back by bad weather, they set off again on Tuesday, 4 June. They were now on their own, in a remote spot and on a serious climb, their only contact with the outside world being non-climbing Richard Hawkins, down at Base Camp.

They climbed to the high point of their first attempt and found the equipment they had cached in a snow hole. The snow hole itself had been destroyed in an avalanche and Simon and Joe were lucky to recover their gear. In view of the avalanche danger at this spot, they dug out a safer snow cave to the south, which was also closer to the face.

The route began up an avalanche cone which was fortunately consolidated. The climbing proper then started with a bang. It was unrelentingly steep and an icefield which they ascended was a constant 80°. They slanted to the right as they climbed and the angle eased to about 65–70°, then got through a rock band via a steep twenty-metre cascade pitch of ice.

Difficulty after difficulty presented itself, often with avalanche risk. To the right a 300-metre yellow rock wall dropped to the base of the icefield. Their problem was to get across this wall by a ramp, access to which was blocked by séracs. It was dark by the time they got to a very steep fall of ice at the foot of a secondary ramp line.

But there were no bivvy sites, so Joe carried on up this. It started as overhanging honeycombed ice for about eight metres, and thereafter was hard ice leading up through a galaxy of large icicles. This pitch was vertical in places and exited in a frightening funnel pitch on to a snow gully. Simon came up then and led through. They were amazed to see on the left of the gully a twenty-metre-diameter 'golf ball' of snow just stuck on to the face, apparently defying the force of gravity. Fate smiled on them now, for they found a huge natural cave inside.

In the morning the difficulties continued unrelenting. From the cave they traversed right and fought their way up another cascade of ice at a high angle. After a further pitch, they at last managed to get on to the main ramp, their key to the higher part of the route.

The ramp was in fact an enormous hanging gully with fortifications at each end in the form of séracs and cornices. Getting there had been desperate and by the looks of things getting out at the other end would be equally exacting. Now they did a rope length to the right, followed by 250 metres up the left side of the gully. This wasn't so steep, between 50° and 60°, by far the easiest climbing so far.

They stopped to take stock of this next problem: the exit from the gully ramp. There was a broken rock wall on the left with a nasty icefall running down parallel with the gully. This looked just possible if they avoided some large icicles on its left, but the snow and ice looked like unstable nougat.

It was Simon who started up this pitch, thrutching up the rotten snow which was plastered at a high angle, but he had to give up after fifteen metres and abseiled from an icicle – not the most reassuring anchor. He next moved left on to the rock face in the hope that this would get him high enough to make a traverse into the gully beyond the ice. He managed to insert a Friend, (a cam-type device which he used as a running belay) and was about three or four metres above it when both of his handholds came away and he peeled off the rock. It was his good Friend which possibly saved his life.

The two young men were now faced with the last option in this dicey trinity. They would have to climb the icicles direct. With care, Joe took the lead up the overhanging ice, and soon it eased to vertical, when he paused for an instant, hanging by the wrist loop of his ice axe. With his other hand he put in an ice peg called a Snarg. It was then a matter of smashing a mass of icicles to enable him to get over this crux. Whilst engaged in this risky occupation he cut his chin. He made a rush to climb the remainder of the steep section which was strenuous and hard. Beyond lay an eighty-metre ice funnel which led to a ridge, a ridge both sharp and airy.

Simon came up and Joe then led on, traversing once more to the right, looking for a way through to the top. It was hair-raising stuff, the basic material for future nightmares. He was back on rock now, it was loose as well as being covered with crappy snow. Tantalisingly, he could see the summit cornices less than 300 metres from him, but en route were ghastly steep powder snow-flutings, like a ploughed field, huge furrows tilted at a ridiculous angle. They found that once in a chosen channel it was almost impossible to change lanes. Just a hundred metres of this took all of five hours!

They felt like high-altitude navvies, forcing a trench up the trough in the flutings. Darkness overtook them and it was two tired, worried climbers who excavated a snow hole on the side of their chosen 'flute'. It had been a frustrating and dangerous section, possibly worse for the second man who could do nothing but sit on his insecure bucket seat excavated from the loose snow and be covered in a cascade of spindrift sent down by his partner, who struggled up to his armpits forging the deep trench.

They were forced to spend the night in their unstable snow hole, hoping that it wouldn't collapse beneath them: to go any higher that night would have been suicidal.

The next morning was 7 June. They were poised for the push to the summit which was only 150 metres away, but despite starting just after first light they didn't top the summit cornice until 2.00 p.m., relieved to be off those horrible flutings.

They stayed on the top for half an hour, taking photographs. Then gathering clouds to the east told them that it was time to move. They studied their way down, by the North Ridge. As this route had been first climbed by a German party in 1936, Joe and Simon had assumed it would not present them with too many difficulties but, seeing it now, they knew better. It looked horrendous, sweeping away to bristling cornices overhanging the West Face.

They set off down but were soon enveloped in thick cloud.

Simon takes up the story:

Shortly after starting the descent we were engulfed in cloud and snow, and lost contact with the ridge. At this point I became completely disoriented and was trying to lead Joe in totally the wrong direction. Fortunately Joe's argument to go the other way prevailed and after a lot of nasty traversing through flutings at the top of Siula Grande's East Face, we saw the ridge again through a break in the cloud. I led up towards it and when I was about thirty feet from the crest an ominous cracking sound filled my ears. This was instantly followed by a falling sensation and the thought that we were both going to die. After what seemed to be a very long time the falling stopped and I was left hanging upside down with an unnerving view of the West Face beneath me. It didn't take long to realise that I'd stepped through a huge cornice. I climbed back up and informed Joe that I'd found the ridge! The event only served to emphasise the dangerous and unstable nature of our chosen descent route.

The ridge continued to be an assortment of snow mushrooms, steep flutings and occasional crevasses. The stress involved in descending it was immense. The fear was suppressed slightly by the concentration required for this technical 'down climbing' and it left me with an uneasy feeling. The day came to an end with about a third of the ridge behind us. The wildest bivouac on the route, a snow hole in a near vertical fluting, did little to relieve my uneasiness.

Joe was in the front now, leading down the ridge, and he describes what happened:

I had thought that the worst of the ridge had been completed but soon found that this was not the case. It became very tortuous with large powder cornices and steep knife-edged ridges. It was not possible to keep below the line of cornices owing to the fluted and unstable powder slopes on the east side.

We descended roped together fifty metres apart. The climbing was never technically hard but always extremely precarious and very tense. Towards eleven o'clock the worst was past and the ridge now formed large solid broad whalebacked cornices. Simon was out of sight as I contoured round the first large cornice and approached the second one. Beyond the ridge dropped to our West Face descent point.

I was surprised to find an ice cliff on the other side of the cornice. This was about fifteen feet high at the crest of the ridge and nearly forty feet high further down the East Face. It wasn't possible to abseil, as the snow on top was unstable and the ridge too dangerous to attempt. I therefore began traversing the cliff edge looking for a weakness, an ice ramp or a crevasse, by which I hoped to get down the cliff.

Suddenly a large section of the edge broke away beneath me and I fell twenty feet on to the slope of the East Face, and then somersaulted down. I knew I had broken my leg in the severe impact as my crampons hit hard ice.

Simon knew that Joe had fallen by the tug on the rope and he was worried:

The reality of the predicament did not come home to me until I had done the precarious abseil to where Joe was. I got out some painkillers from my rucksack and gave them to him. His right leg was quite obviously broken. My immediate thoughts were that the situation was quite hopeless and that Joe was as good as dead. But eventually I realised that I would have to make some kind of effort to try and get him off the mountain.

I traversed back towards the ridge and saw that reasonably angled snow slopes led down to the Col Santa Rosa. Fortunately Joe's accident had occurred on the last technical part of the ridge. After returning to him, I then climbed up to free the abseil ropes which had stuck. While I was doing this Joe managed to traverse towards the ridge on his own.

Getting back up to the abseil point was for me the most frightening part of the epic. It involved climbing the ice cliff at its lowest point. This place, unfortunately, also happened to be on the corniced edge of the ridge. Climbing the ice solo took a very long time with terrifying views of Siula Grande's West Face viewed through fracture lines in the cornice. When I reached the anchor point I made sure the doubled rope would now run freely and abseiled again. There was no trouble this time and the rope pulled down easily. I then caught up with Joe who was making slow and painful progress.

I'm not exactly sure whose idea it was, but a system for

lowering Joe was devised. The two fifty-metre ropes were tied together. I sat in a seat-shaped platform dug out of the snow and started lowering Joe through a Sticht plate, a friction device. After fifty metres the knot which joined the two ropes together reached the plate. Now Joe took his weight off the rope so that I could swap the knot to the other side of the plate and lower him a further fifty metres. I then down-climbed to him and as I was doing his he cut a platform for me to belay from for the next lower. While I was lowering, Joe would lie on his left side to stop his broken right leg from being jarred. Even so it was obviously very painful but I only stopped lowering him when the pain was intense, because of the urgency of getting him off the mountain.

Joe recalls:
Simon was very much in control and all I had to do was cope with the pain and execute any manoeuvres as safely as possible. We both began to feel optimistic about getting to the glacier and the sanctuary of a snow hole that night. We worked well as a team and made steady progress down the 650-metre face. Already Simon had lowered me 200 metres to the col.

By nightfall we reckoned we were only two and a half rope lengths from the glacier. On what should have been the second-last lower, disaster hit when I was lowered accidentally over an ice cliff. The situation suddenly changed from possible to hopeless. When the lowering ropes reached halfway point at the belay plate I was hanging free fifty feet above a huge crevasse!

Simon, who could not now see Joe, was also in a desperate situation:
After about fifty feet the rope came tight, and I knew Joe had gone over a steeper section. I carried on lowering until the knot in the rope came up and gave tugs on the rope to tell Joe to take his weight off the rope.

Joe did not respond. I carried on tugging at the rope and screaming for Joe to do something. As time went by my screaming became more desperate. I was getting very cold. My already frostbitten hands were getting worse, my legs were going numb and the snow seat was gradually collapsing.

Back to Joe:

This, I thought was the end. I was exhausted and very cold, and felt cheated, as if something was determined to finish me off, irrespective of what we tried to do to prevent it. I was giving up the ghost.

In darkness, with avalanches pouring off the cliff edge above, a strong biting wind and a temperature of $-20°C$, I felt too numbed to attempt anything. My efforts at prusiking failed as one of my frozen hands dropped a loop and I felt too shattered afterwards to do any more.

I distinctly remember thinking of Toni Kurtz who was left hanging on a rope from an overhang on the North Wall of the Eiger. He froze to death. I thought that at last I knew what he must have felt like. Approaching death wasn't as bad as the books led me to think. I tried and failed – tough shit! I was spinning from my waist harness, too weak to hold myself upright, and I could see in my mind's eye that horrific old black and white photograph of Kurtz's corpse on the rope with long icicles hanging from the points of his crampons. My legs were numb and I was grateful because I could feel no pain now. I wondered if Simon would die with me and if anyone would ever find us.

The longer I hung there, the more relaxed I felt about everything, even feeling quite calm about knowing I was going to die fairly soon. In a lazy sort of way it didn't really bother me, seemed to have nothing to do with Joe Simpson. It was just a fact of life – of death.

Simon must have had a terrible time on the slope above struggling to hold on to me and realising his belay seat was collapsing beneath him and all the time being in the full force of the avalanches.

Simon's predicament was indeed desperate. He realised that if he didn't do something soon they would both perish.

I remembered Joe had given me his Swiss Army knife for cutting abseil slings. After getting the knife out of my rucksack I cut Joe's rope. It seemed a very rational thing to do and I did it very calmly.

On the end of the rope Joe must have known that what was about to occur was the only logical solution:

When I felt myself slip several inches I realised what was about to happen. I wondered whether he would be able to cut himself free in time. I looked down and knew I wouldn't survive a free fall into the crevasse.

I was looking up the rope when I suddenly felt myself hurtling down. I wasn't scared, more confused. I hit the snow roof of the crevasse very hard and twisted sideways as I broke through it, then accelerated down again. I couldn't see but felt all the snow roof cascading past. Further down I hit a snow bridge in the crevasse on my side – very hard – and banged my knee, which made me cry out.

It took me a long time to recover and sit up. I think my left hip had been dislocated because when I moved it popped back in. I could only feel my knee at the time.

Simon had now to act quickly or he could freeze to death on the exposed face:

I immediately set about digging a snow hole as it was necessary to get into my sleeping bag as quickly as possible. Excavating the hole took a very long time. My mind was full of quite bizarre thoughts. At first they were speculative: what had happened to Joe? I knew we were nearly on the glacier and hoped Joe had not fallen on to the avalanche chute leading to this. I wondered if the fall had injured him further and if he could survive the night. Eventually I became convinced that my action was bound to have resulted in Joe's death. I got into my sleeping bag and felt terrible. My mind was working at an incredible rate, jumping from one subject to another. Occasionally I would smell the water in the surrounding snow and wish for a drink. Eventually I had a little sleep.

Joe, after his fall:

That Sunday night in the crevasse was the worst thing I've ever experienced in my life, for I suffer slightly from claustrophobia. The first thing I did was put an ice peg into the side wall of the crevasse and tie myself to it. Then I looked around with my torch. There seemed no way out but up. The roof I came through was about fifty feet above. It was impossible to climb up there but in desperation I tried four times before giving up.

I'm sure I went mad from about 11.00 p.m. to 3.00 a.m. and I was convinced that Simon thought me dead. I had no reason to presume this, I just felt it in my bones. It was a living nightmare, a turmoil of thoughts ricocheting within my head.

I reckoned it could take me days to die in that crevasse. I've never felt so isolated and abandoned in my life. I seriously thought of untying and jumping down the hole to my left into the bowels of the ice, but I knew I wouldn't be able to do it. I just huddled up against the ice wall like a frightened child and cried, shouted, moaned and generally felt very sorry for myself. I then tried to rationalise, thinking that we all have to die some time and that this was just my time, this was my way. I wondered how many others had died in a similar way and what they had done and how they had coped. It felt strange to think I was now just another one of those reports you see in Mountain Accident statistics. I had now an awful realisation of what all those tales of climbers' deaths in the mountains really meant. I felt sad for all of them.

This went on and on, recurring thoughts, getting nowhere. I had deliberately not got into my pit – my sleeping bag or my bivvy sack. At about 3.00 a.m. a wave of anger and resentment swept over me and I made a resolute effort to control myself. I decided, fuck it, I've got this far, why give up now? Maybe in the morning I'll see a way out. I never once believed that Simon would find me or get me out. It was as if I had banished him from my mind. When I did struggle into my sleeping bag it was with the greatest difficulty. The pain was intense but eventually I did get some disjointed sleep.

I awoke about 6.00 a.m. and at once started screaming, 'Simon . . . Simon.' I felt dehydrated and it was difficult to shout. But no sign of Simon, perhaps he too had fallen? He wouldn't be able to see me where I was and maybe my voice was too weak.

Dawn for Simon wasn't a bed of roses either:

When I awoke it was still dark and I began to think about getting down to Base Camp. This made me very afraid. I was quite convinced that I would be killed as a form of retribution. When it got light I packed my rucksack and geared up, very slowly and meticulously as though it was a sort of peculiar last ceremony.

After getting out of the snow hole I saw the slope beneath ended in a cliff edge and below that the avalanche chute led down on to the glacier. I traversed rightwards above the cliff towards a couloir that I could see would bring me down on to the glacier. Once in the couloir I had to abseil and as I went down the doubled rope I could see across to the ice cliff that I had lowered Joe over. At the bottom of it was a huge crevasse. Joe had obviously fallen into it. I shouted, 'Joe, Joe,' while abseiling, but I was totally convinced that he was dead, and didn't bother going over to the crevasse.

Walking back across the glacier was tiring due to the deep snow and my general condition. Only when I reached the moraine was I convinced of my own survival. I began thinking then of how to break the news to Richard at Base Camp. I realised that I could fabricate a less controversial story to tell him and later other people, but I dismissed this idea immediately, knowing that I was simply not capable of it.

Coming over the final moraine before Base Camp I met Richard on his way up to look for us. I told him Joe was dead and explained how it came about. In a very subdued mood we went back to base.

Joe in the bowels of the ice decided to get to grips with his situation:

Look around, I told myself, see what it's like. Is there a way out? Not up, impossible, not left, not right. Hang on. I can see a ledge. Is it a false bottom to the crevasse eighty feet down? There's light on it. Maybe there is an exit from down there, I rambled on. No. Can't go down deeper, don't want to go down. But what if that snow floor is just a thin cover? I'll never get back up to this ledge again.

I pulled the rope down from the blocks of snow in the roof above and saw the frayed end of nylon fibres. Seeing it sort of made my mind up for me, as if it confirmed the situation that I was in and forced me to face facts. If there was no escape down there then it would make no difference to me now. I was going to die if I stayed here so what difference would it make if I did so eighty feet lower? It was Hobson's choice but I still cringed from going down. It might mean a quick death if I fell and I wasn't as prepared for that as I had thought.

In the end I weighted the frayed end of the rope with karabiners and abseiled down. Once on this lower snow bridge or platform, I was delighted to find that the floor was reasonably solid though I didn't detach myself from the rope.

I could see holes going deep down on the outer side of the

29

crevasse, so obviously it continued beneath what I was lying on. The floor must have been made by avalanches pouring in from above and they had formed a powder cone rising right up to the roof which began about twenty or thirty feet in front of me. At the top I could see a small circular hole, head width, with a column of gold sunlight angling in on to the back wall of the slot. Seeing this gave me the most incredible lift. All the time I was in the crevasse and especially then at its deepest point I had the most overwhelming sense of isolation and of being completely cut off and abandoned. It was the eeriest feeling, all light blue and shadowed, everything totally lifeless, like being in a crypt, where nothing living had ever been or would ever come again.

That shaft of sun however dispelled all this and gave me a link with the outside world, even though I had great doubts if I would be able to climb the slope, knowing how hard the climbing had been for me up above.

The angle was about 50° at the bottom, gradually steepening to 60° near the roof and in the region of twenty-five feet wide at the base and six feet broad at the top. I crawled over to it, still tied to the abseil rope fixed to the ice peg eighty feet above. It was very soft powder and after much faffing around I sorted out a system by which I could tackle it. I cut out then stamped down a small platform-step with another step just below it to the right, then I hefted my bad leg into this and with axes and armpits buried deeply above, executed a big hop to get my good leg on to the platform, then I lifted my injured leg up to it as well and started all over again.

The pitch was about 130 feet and when I got higher the abseil rope hung almost horizontal behind me. The steeper it got the more precarious and strenuous it became to step up. Several times near the top I very nearly fell off.

After six hours of this hell I popped my head out through the roof exit and saw before me all the world. My world. The feeling of exultation was quite indescribable. I couldn't believe that I had done it. I could see the glacier about 150 feet below me and the route back to camp. I was yelling and shouting like a mad thing, just shouting for no reason except perhaps relief. I wanted to cry but couldn't.

It was about 12.30 p.m. on a bright sunny day. When I

reached the glacier, I knew that Simon had returned presuming me dead. I saw his tracks and started to crawl after them. The rest was just crawling. For another three days I clawed my way down, getting weaker each day. Despite being out of it a lot of the time, hallucinating on the glacier, talking to myself, shouting then shouting some more, I just kept going mechanically, detached, like an automaton. I was very methodical about it. I am surprised in retrospect how controlled I was, fixing stages to reach, not thinking beyond them, snow holing and bivouacking when I wanted to keep going on yet knew the weather would kill me if I did. I know that if I had been in that situation at eighteen, I would not have survived. There was a lot of experience in me that made me do the right thing at the right time.

By far the hardest thing was being alone, having no one to talk to or to encourage me. The great temptation was to just lie still and say sod it, I'm going to sleep for a while. It was so hard to fight on my own. This was especially so the two days on the boulder field when I fell a lot; I always seemed to be lying still, waiting for pain to subside.

I had continuous conversations with myself as if I were talking with another person. On the last day, 11 June, I saw Simon's and Richard's footprints in the mud and was convinced that they were with me. There was an uncanny sense of someone else following along quietly. It felt very comforting. I was absolutely sure for about three hours that Richard was in front and Simon behind, out of sight because they didn't want me to be embarrassed by my condition, but encouraging me along. When I fell over and it hurt badly they didn't come to help. I thought it was because they wanted me to do this thing by myself and that seemed all right, really. I was just glad that they were there and someone knew I wasn't dead.

Suddenly the bubble burst and I knew they had never been there and that I was alone and dead as far as they were concerned. That came as quite a blow to me mentally.

Until halfway through the third day dehydration was very bad. I had had no water or food since Sunday night. It now was Tuesday and I felt terrible. I couldn't raise saliva and my tongue was swollen and dry. I had trouble breathing evenly, always being excessively out of breath. When I got to water I drank litres and litres. It tasted like nectar and at once I began to feel stronger and had less trouble breathing.

I knew having no food was bad but didn't miss it and I was very much aware that I was getting progressively weaker and slower. That last, usually ten-minute, walk to camp took me six and a half hours! I could just shuffle a bit and then lie back shattered. I've never felt so fucked in my life.

Simon and Richard were meanwhile packing up camp:

The night before we had arranged to leave, just as it was getting dark, I heard a distant cry that sounded like 'Simon'. I thought little of it as there had been a few locals about tending to their cattle. But Richard and I were awakened shortly after midnight by a clear call of 'Simon, help me.'

We shot out of our sleeping bags and dashed outside the tent. It was an eerie sight that greeted us. The night was misty with gently falling snow. Joe was slumped on a rock about fifty yards from the tent. He was in an appalling physical state. His face was incredibly thin, his eyes sunken, he was covered in mud, stank of fleas and urine, with a smell of acetone on his breath from starvation.

Joe said later:

I believe that was as far as I would have got. When Simon's and Richard's torches came bobbing across the snow everything seemed to drain out of me; all the fight which had kept me going evaporated. There was no longer a need to boost myself, now others would help. I felt myself just give up and pain came rushing in, the exhaustion, everything. I sometimes wonder if that wasn't the point at which I was most at risk, whether I could suddenly just have keeled over and died. I felt like death, and no doubt smelt like it as well.

At this point a helicopter would have been an answer to prayer, but this was not the Alps or Glencoe. It was one of the remoter corners of the High Andes, and evacuating Joe Simpson involved a tortuous haggling first with muleteers, then with police in the nearest town, followed by a truck ride to Lima with an obliviously drunken driver, before Joe was deposited in hospital three days later. He was not yet rid of the trauma of his ghastly experience and in hospital during pre-sedation had one more of those weird dreams he had suffered during the long nights and agonising days after the accident.

Joe:

I was back in the crevasse again and a passage from Shakespeare's *Measure for Measure* came to mind where a condemned man contemplates execution. I had had to learn it about fifteen years before and hadn't seen or even thought about it since. It was a dream with words. When I woke up I wrote it on my plaster cast:

> Death is a fearful thing . . .
> . . . To die, and go we know not where;
> To lie in cold obstruction, and to rot;
> This sensible warm motion to become
> A kneaded clod; and the delighted spirit
> To bathe in fiery floods or to reside
> In thrilling region of thick-ribbed ice . . .

3

FROM PILLAR TO PEAK

A Dru Trilogy

Because it is so overcrowded and offers so many testing climbs, the Mont Blanc massif is one of the world's blackest spots as far as mountain accidents are concerned. In both winter and summer climbers flock to the Chamonix area. It is a testing ground for higher regions, such as the Andes and Himalaya, as well as a mountain playground in its own right.

There are many dramatic and horrific tales to tell from this wonderful region, but with the help of my friend Emmanuel Schmutz, who was an active member of the Chamonix rescue team, I have included three stories which all took place on the Petit Dru, a slender mountain of great beauty and one of which I have vivid personal memories, as my first narrative will explain.

No Head for Heights

My own tangle with the Petit Dru was in 1958. My climbing companion was Chris Bonington. We had first met up in 1953 in Scotland where we had launched assaults on hitherto unclimbed gullies and faces and later in 1957 had made a short-lived attempt on the Eiger North Wall, a route then unclimbed by a British party.

Our quixotic sortie on the flanks of the Eiger had only served to whet my appetite for Alpine firsts, but had had the opposite effect on Chris. He wanted to get an established route or two under his belt, not waste his time chasing dazzling possibilities and great last problems. So when we took up residence in a tumbledown goat herder's hut at Montenvers the following season there was a constant running argument between us, me holding out objectives like the Shroud on the Grandes Jorasses, Chris muttering about suicide routes and Highland idiots. As the weather was desperate, with heavy early-season snow, much of the great debate was academic anyway. So we sat there reasonably amicably tucking into army compo rations left over from Chris's last tour of duty with his tank crew in Germany. My contribution to the catering was for some reason twenty-five pounds of figs and a gallon of molasses, an unfortunate choice for the general atmosphere of the hut and one necessitating frequent nocturnal dashes to the shrubbery.

We eventually settled on a compromise. When the weather lifted I agreed to go on a training climb before we ventured on more serious objectives. We made the ascent profitable by de-pegging the route, that is to say, extracting all but the essential pitons, thereby making it a more enjoyable ascent for those who were to follow and bringing our ironmongery reserves up to scratch. Such is the logic of the impecunious.

Now, with a known climb under our waist loops, it was my turn, and I suggested a new line to Chris on the Pointe de Lépiney.

'Just the thing for you, Chris, bugger-all snow and lovely warm smooth granite.'

'I'll believe it when I see it,' he muttered.

Our stepping stone for this enterprise was the Envers des Aiguilles Hut, perched crazily on the south side of the Charmoz like a fairy castle, though perhaps squarer in profile. It still boasted a beautiful princess in the form of the custodian's daughter, the only person in residence. No doubt dutifully remembering the 'Auld Alliance' she took me under her wing, much to Chris's chagrin.

Our new route lived up to Chris's worst fears. Our attempt turned out to be a fiasco. We soon discovered that the reason it hadn't been climbed was because it bristled with overhangs. On one of these, after we had a frigid bivouac, Chris fell. He didn't injure himself, and consequently went back at it again with the determination of a Jack Russell terrier. He got up, only to find other overhangs sprouting above, even more menacing than the one just vanquished. After a meeting of the partnership we decided to retreat with what dignity we could muster, and I had the bright idea of descending a couloir which seemed to be the shortest distance between two points – our present position and the glacier a thousand feet below.

In an hour we were in the innards of a horrendous chimney with water beating on our heads. I had gone down first and was hanging from a peg which I had inserted with difficulty. When Chris joined me to share the only mini-foothold, we found that the abseil rope had jammed. Showing great fortitude Chris went up the rope using the painstaking technique of prusiking, a special sliding knot which locks when weight is put on it.

The final sting in the tail of this Aiguille route was a rimaye at least ten feet wide. That's a gap between snowfield and rock face. When I abseiled down, Chris was ensconced on a mantelshelf-sized ledge above this intimidating slot like an eaglet contemplating its first flight. As the rope was long enough, I continued past him, kicking out from the last nose of rock on an overhang, and just managed to reach the snow on the far lip of the gap. It was a hairy business.

Bedraggled, we slunk down, pride hurt and bodies aching with this abortive encounter. The two young knights who peacocked about the Aiguilles de l'Envers Hut on the way up now stole furtively past the door in case the shapely *gardienne* should spot us. Finally, to make bad worse we lost our way among the crevasses of the Mer de Glace in the dark, and what normally takes half an hour took us three.

We had now been joined in our hut by two young Austrians, after whom our abode would eventually be known as the Chalet Austria. Walter Philip was twenty-one, tall and dark with panther-lithe movements; Richard Blach, three years younger, was quiet and slightly built. Despite their youth they had done some impressive climbs in the Eastern Alps. Chris and I immediately struck up a friendship with them and we pooled our gastronomic resources. The diet of the two Austrians was almost as monotonous as ours. They had arrived with rucksacks bristling with salami and very little else. As they feared for the lifespan of their protein cylinders,

I suggested they use the Mer de Glace as a refrigerator. With due solemnity they lowered the salami into the depths of a crevasse, not before I had made an exchange for some figs and molasses, and the nocturnal atmosphere deteriorated accordingly.

At last the sun struggled out and Chris and I reached an honourable solution as to our major objective. I proposed what was still regarded as probably the most serious rock climb in the Alps at the time, the Bonatti Pillar of the Petit Dru. First climbed by Walter Bonatti, who had done it in a breathtaking solo lasting five days in 1953, the South-West Pillar had been climbed four times since, but none of the parties had been British. I knew it would tempt Chris.

'The Pillar's right up your alley,' I encouraged. 'Rock most of the way and good rock at that.'

It was agreed and Walter and Richard would make it a foursome. The previous year Walter had made a fast ascent of the West Face of the Petit Dru, a 3000-foot sweep of smooth featureless granite which borders on the Pillar, and so he knew the way down, always a reassuring factor should the weather take a turn for the worse.

We were, however, at a loss where to obtain a description of the Bonatti Pillar and descended to Chamonix to recruit Donald Snell, a local sport-shop owner, to obtain this for us. We succeeded. After steak and chips at the Bar Nationale we hiked back up the cog railway to Montenevers and our shack.

This (1958) was before the days of routine helicopter monitoring, where parties are often checked each evening from the air to see if they are all right. An accident on such a climb as the Bonatti Pillar was too awful for us to contemplate, but we made a simple arrangement with the station-master at Montenvers next day as we left with laden sacks. We would give him a torch signal to record our progress on the climb. 'Every night at nine o'clock, André.'

There was a great feeling of relief in leaving the penned-in area of Montenvers where hundreds of multi-coloured tourists gaze at the mountains and cluster round the large pay-and-look telescopes.

We crossed the dirty slug of the Mer de Glace and climbed the steep moraine on the far bank – a hazardous business as it was then a cliff of scree. The normal bivouac for the start of both the West Face and the Bonatti route is the Rognon du Dru, a pleasantly located rock 'dwelling' comprising an overhang which, if the wind is from the right quarter, and it doesn't rain or snow, offers one-star comfort for uncomplaining alpinists.

Just before dusk we saw two figures approaching with large rucksacks. As they came closer we could see that one was almost as broad as he was tall. Like me he wore a flat cap. We immediately recognised him as Don Whillans, one of the foremost climbers of his generation and probably the greatest British alpinist ever. It was Don who had made the first British ascent of the West Face with Joe Brown. His companion now was Paul Ross, one of the English Lake District's star climbers. They had long French loaves fingering from their packs.

'How do,' Don spoke. It was a gruff but neutral-sounding greeting, neither friendly nor aggressive. He gave his home-rolled fag a drag and studied us with his small beady eyes, obviously weighing us up.

'Hello, Don,' Chris responded. 'Heading for the Bonatti?'

'That's right, Chris.' Don looked steadily at me. 'I hear that you have a description of the Bonatti, Hamish.' It sounded as if I had just filched some classified documents. 'I was in at Snell's,' he added, explaining how he had gleaned this intelligence.

'Not much of a description, Don,' I returned. 'You know Bonatti is as tight with his route descriptions as a Yorkshire-man with brass!'

'Aye. Well, we'll be seeing you.' Don gave another draw on his cigarette. 'It looks as if this doss is fully booked so we'll mosey up higher to see if we can find somewhere to bivvy.'

We set the alarm for 2.00 a.m. and settled down for what sleep we could get. But that early reveille, shared by bakers and alpinists, proved to be cloudy, so we turned over and Chris soon announced with snores that he was at peace with the world.

By 5.30 a.m. the weather looked better and I gave him a shake.

'Wake up, fella, time to move.' The Austrians were already up and Walter was champing at the bit.

'Could be a good day, Walter,' I greeted, 'even though we'll be keeping office hours.'

'Ja, Hammish, we will have much fun.'

I was later to reflect on this observation.

As we entered the jaws of the couloir we could see two small figures above. Don and Paul were already roped up, but when we reached the rimaye between the lower snowfield and the rocky start to the couloir, Walter suggested that we should climb unroped to save time. We agreed, which proved to be a somewhat foolhardy decision. For, preparing to make the long stride from the snow to gain the rock, Walter fell when the lip of unstable snow which he was standing on collapsed. He instinctively threw himself backwards thereby avoiding a rapid and chilly descent into the hole. Undeterred, he jumped across and raced up the rock on the other side as if he was in four-wheel drive. There was a lot of grit and stones on the smooth granite which made it very treacherous.

In a short time we had caught up with Don and Paul and it was the classic hare and tortoise fable. Don was leading and Walter clambered past him as if he was in the fast lane, with a brief 'Good Morning'.

When Walter was just above the stoic Mancunian, he slipped and fell on top of Don, who only with considerable effort arrested Walter's fall. It was a close thing and I thought Don was most restrained. The MacInnes, Bonington, Philip, Blach combine belatedly decided to rope up!

So we emerged at the wall of the Flammes de Pierre which effectively blocks off the top of the couloir. I had been pushed into the lead for the previous few hours on the false assumption that I could cut endless steps in the hard ice. The top of the couloir was steep snow and ice and as there was only one pair of crampons in our party, steps were essential.

From the cold dark depths of the couloir, we could see the Pillar above wrapped in a golden brown with sunshine. We were elated, just as Druids must have felt when addressing the dawn.

In a slot in the rock at the very base of the Pillar, we found a walking stick, as if it had been placed in a hallstand. We never did find out who left it there. Here was the sun, its warm rays probing our bodies and rejuvenating us. But there was work to do, 2000 feet of it, some of the most intimidating rock climbing in the Alps. Don now came into his own and for me it was the start of a long association from which my respect for him as a master alpinist grew.

'Aye, well,' he drawled, 'I think you, Walter, and your mate Richard should go in front and Paul and I can follow behind and give you a spell if you get tired.'

'Zat is all right by us,' Walter responded eagerly.

'Fine. Paul and I can do the sack-hauling up the pitches and Hamish and you, Chris, can take up the rear de-pegging.'

'Suits me, Don, I've got the "Message".' I brandished my large piton hammer made in a Clydeside shipyard.

In minutes the Austrians had vanished like inspired chamois. The climbing was a kaleidoscope of overhangs, cracks, dièdres, slabs and walls, all at crazy angles. None was easy and we realised that this was climbing of a high order. It had taken us five hours to get up the couloir, which was normal, but now on warm rock we were keen to make fast time. We soon concertinaed, however. It was becoming harder and Walter had trouble getting over a large overhang. He did this using an étrier, a short rope ladder, which he clipped into the pegs and wedges in a crack. Don, who was watching this exhibition of gravity defiance, told Paul that he'd start sack-hauling here and he tackled the pitch with deliberation. He climbed it by holding on to the pegs but instead of continuing up the line which the Austrians had taken, which is the normal route, he climbed directly up a groove, a new variation which was desperately hard. When he was above, Don hauled up all our rucksacks and Paul joined him at his stance. When it was Chris's turn to lead this pitch, he had a struggle, but he didn't ask for a top rope, which he could easily have had from Paul. Chris admitted to me later that it was one of the hardest pitches he had ever led. I agreed that it was desperate and I had the security of a top rope when it was my turn, thankful as I thrutched upwards that I hadn't had to lead it.

Above, the climb became very exposed and the void below our climbing boots seemed to have a magnetic quality as if trying to pull us into the depths of the couloir. I could see Don above. He had let Paul lead and somehow both ropes had got threaded through the karabiners with the result that Paul couldn't now haul the rucksacks. Don had two of these on his shoulders and was climbing an overhanging pitch free, with his fingers hooked through the loops of the wedges. We heard him yell for the rope to be taken in, for there was slack, probably caused by friction through the runners. A peg he was holding on to with two fingers of his left hand was slowly coming out, but with a burst of energy he grabbed a small wooden wedge above and succeeded in fighting his way to the stance. He said later that this pitch had caused him more exertion than the rest of the climb put together.

A couple of hundred feet above, there was a pendulum move across the wall from a flake. Actually, it was a tension traverse where we swung across a vertical smooth wall holding on to a short rope secured to a piton above; an exhilarating experience when there's 2000 feet of fresh air beneath boots that don't have anything to stand on.

After a short steep chimney we found ourselves on a luxurious ledge and as it was now late in the afternoon we decided to call it a day. Walter and Richard had gone up some eighty feet to a further small platform, which they informed us was quite adequate for their humble needs.

We consulted our abbreviated bible, Bonatti's description, and discovered that we had made good progress. It was obviously the wise decision to take advantage of this horizontal haven in such blank verticality. Directly above, the rock rose in one mighty sweep as high as the Empire State Building.

One of the fascinating aspects Himalayan and Alpine climbing have in common with hitting your head against a wall is that it's wonderful when you stop. Not that you hate the process of actually climbing, but when you settle down for the night in some airy bivvy, you have time to reflect and collect yourself, and, if it's a good evening, soak in the view. At such times one almost feels like a bird – like Tennyson's eagle, clasping the crags, lord of all you survey. It was such a night on our bivvy ledge on the South-West Pillar. The lights of Chamonix twinkled like a fairground, and across the valley above tourist-deserted Montenvers, the Grepon and Charmoz stood to attention in the twilight. My thoughts took me back to when I was a young lad traversing those peaks solo.

Actually, I was following the famous French guide, Lionel Terray, who allowed me to tag along behind him and his current client. In this way I gained alpine experience and he kept a fatherly eye on me.

That particular excursion, however, had a drastic ending. We had reached the top of the Charmoz and I was following them down in a series of abseils, when the sling I was abseiling from snapped. It had held for both of them. I fell about forty feet, fortunately stopping on a small ledge. Lionel, who was a few hundred feet lower, saw me fall and was with me in ten minutes.

I had injured both feet and my knees had jack-knifed into my eye sockets with the impact, so that I couldn't see. Lionel was obviously going to require help to get me down and after ascertaining that I could descend on a rope, decided to get me below the main difficulties and then go for help. He couldn't abandon his client though, who was looking anxious, no doubt concerned at being left on his own.

With Lionel telling me where hand and footholds were, I moved down stiffly and painfully. I could face in all right, but couldn't put weight on my heels. I could just see through a red film; but we both realised that I would have to be carried back to Montenvers. I couldn't walk on level ground. Lionel spotted the guide Raymond Lambert on the Grepon and shouted to him to come and assist. In some twenty minutes Raymond and an aspirant guide joined us. In such distinguished company I had made steady progress back down to Montenvers.

My ruminations were cut short by the need to make our 9.00 p.m. signal to our friendly stationmaster. In a few minutes answering flashes winked up at us. It was comforting to know that down there, across the Mer de Glace, someone cared and took the trouble to keep in touch.

Don and Paul also had their stove roaring and the aroma of soup and compo wafted luxuriously around the Pillar. It was so peaceful. I can still recall thinking that when there was a hideous cacophony of falling rocks; they were below, piling into the couloir, sending up showers of sparks. They took ages to sweep down the rock and ice of this bowling alley and presently the appetising smell of soup was replaced by the pungent smell of brimstone, a smell to me associated with death and destruction.

'Just as well that bloody lot didn't roll this morning,' Don remarked drily, 'there wouldn't have been much of us left.'

All was quiet again, even more so after that shattering interlude. Then a high-pitched whine, like a ricochet from a sniper's bullet, cut through the silence. It had that confident, predestined note, which we all felt meant it was destined for us. I was the prime target. The rock bit into my scalp like a blow from a stone axe, catapulting me forward under its impact so that I was left hanging from my belay. Momentarily I was stunned. Instinctively my hands went to my head and I could feel warm blood oozing between my fingers. I can't remember a great deal of what happened next, but I gather that Chris, who had a wound dressing in his rucksack, pressed it over the gash to stem the bleeding and tied it under my chin.

Seating arrangements were changed and we all huddled back against the wall of the pillar, out of range of any other stray missiles. I was poised above Chris in a shallow groove and several times during the night I slumped unconscious on top of him. It was cold and I for one was in no state to think of tomorrow, but the others did. There was no question of retreat, the couloir was just too dangerous and it would have been difficult to abseil down the Pillar in any case, due to the traverses we made on the ascent.

In the morning we unfolded like newly exhumed zombies, our joints cold and stiff.

Chris asked, 'How are you feeling, Hamish?'

'Not a bundle of fun, Chris, but I'll get by.' I must have looked a mess, for Richard, who was above, sharing a perch with Walter, turned pale when he first looked down.

We had a brew and Chris suggested that Don should rope up with me as he was the strongest member of the party.

'I'll take out the pegs with Paul, Don.'

'Aye, all right,' Don looked thoughtful. 'That may be the best policy. You think you'll make it, Mac?'

'I'll have a go,' I said, trying to muster confidence. 'Not many alternatives, are there?'

The Austrians had already started and the ring of pegs being driven home echoed from the rock. Walter was fighting his way up a line of grooves which scored the otherwise smooth face of the Pillar. It was climbing of a high order and Walter demonstrated his talent for pegging by inserting each new peg at the absolute limit of his reach, and he was tall. Sometimes it was possible to get finger jams and if it hadn't been for my nocturnal mishap I could even have enjoyed it. As it was, from time to time I could feel the Dru and my surroundings slipping away from me as I lapsed into wonderful unconsciousness where, for a minute or so, all was peaceful. Don played me like a sluggish fish, not giving me an inch of slack and exerting a persistent and welcome tension, and on the hardest sections literally hauling me up.

I looked up to where Walter and Richard were spreadeagled on the smooth red wall. For the last half-hour Walter had been requesting more and more pegs.

'That's the bloody lot,' Don yelled up as he tied on the last six pitons which Chris had extracted below – a strenuous and frustrating task.

'You watch my rope, Hamish, if you can, and I'll take a mosey round the corner to the right, there must be a bloody easier way than up there.'

In a couple of minutes he came into view again, a small broad figure with his large rucksack making him look like a hunchback gorilla.

'It's this way,' he jerked a thumb, a wide grin on his face, 'up the biggest overhang in the three kingdoms.'

When I went round to join him I saw this was no exaggeration. A great roof hung over the face up which ran a crack punctuated with wooden wedges in various degrees of decay. My heart seemed to stop, for I realised that I just didn't have the reserves to climb it.

Walter was recalled, de-pegging the long pitch as he abseiled. He had put a tremendous amount of work into attempting that terrifying red wall, all to no avail.

I secured myself to a small chockstone in a daze and craned my neck backwards to where Don was now swinging from the wedges. It seemed as easy for him as climbing stairs. I had to give up watching after a time, for it hurt my head. Presently the others joined me on my small ledge.

'What's it like above?' Chris shouted up.

'A bit steep, send up some more pegs.'

'It's getting late,' Chris yelled back. 'It's almost seven o'clock and it'll soon be dark.'

I could see Don looking at his watch.

'I'll come down,' he returned. 'We can bivvy on the ledges where we spent most of the afternoon.'

He pulled the two ropes up through the pegs and lowered them, where they hung out beyond us in space. When he abseiled he had to swing in and Walter fielded him and pulled him on to our ledge.

We climbed down to the wider ledges, feeling despondent that we had made so little progress that day. Don had virtually pulled me up every pitch and I was feeling a burden to the party. But it was a matter of carrying on and not giving up, and I only hoped I would feel stronger in the morning. Chris signalled to the stationmaster, just the usual signal – we were continuing.

It was a night which didn't seem to end.

I huddled in a crack above the others with a peg belay behind me because I didn't want to descend any more than I had to, and Paul sent up my dinner, two bangers, on the rope. Anyhow, I suppose in some ways I fared better on my perch than Chris. He shared Don's bivvy bag and as Don was a chain smoker and Chris a non-smoker, one puffed and the other coughed all night. We hadn't had anything to drink since the previous morning and our throats felt swollen and sore. The cold was insidious, seeking out every chink and gap in our bivvy sacks and, as we were hidden from the morning sun, it took ages to sort out the frozen ropes and to thaw our boots. Breakfast was an oatmeal block which looked and tasted like plastic wood.

Don suggested to Walter that he should lead.

'I'm going to have to help Hamish up this.' He pointed a gloved finger in the direction of the roof. 'It's a bit strenuous.'

I watched Walter climb. He seemed to have tremendous drive and literally threw himself at a climbing problem;

45

usually he got up – but not always. He later told me of his attempt on the North Face of the Cima de Laveredo, when he fell from the second pitch and plunged the total length of the rope, a fall of 300 feet. At the full extension of the nylon he just touched the scree at the base of the climb and escaped with minor injuries. I felt envious as I watched him snap off icicles to suck as he climbed the overhang.

It seemed to take me ages to get up that pitch. Don couldn't give much assistance and from time to time I passed out. It was strange coming to again to find myself swinging from a rope threaded through pegs and wedges – a reversal of the normal nightmare situation, here reality was the nightmare. Chris coming up just behind was a comfort, he described me as 'hanging like a corpse from a gibbet'.

Above the roof was another, but not so overhanging. I was part way up, thanks to Don's persistent tension on the rope, when the sun hit me. It was now the time of day when more sensible people were sitting down to lunch and there was considerable power in those life-giving rays. Before I reached Don's ledge the heat was beginning to get to me and Chris, who was still wearing his duvet jacket, found it almost unbearable. It seemed amazing in so short a span of time to suffer such extremes of temperature.

Paul was behind Chris de-pegging the overhangs. I sat recuperating while Don made a brew using ice he had found in a crack, his dixie piled up with this frozen aggregate, for it had a high gravel content. I heard a call from below and peered over the edge. It was Chris. He had reached a peg on a hard blank pitch and was feeling shattered with the combination of cold, heat and dehydration. He asked for a top rope. In a couple of minutes he had tied on to this and joined us on the ledge, his eyes lighting up when he saw the brew – even if it was only a gritty mouthful each.

It was a strange situation. There was now standing room only, as the ledge was the area of a kitchen chair and with three of us on it everything had to be done by numbers. Walter and Richard were still ahead, and from what Don told us they were having trouble route finding.

Five minutes later we heard a cry from above. It was Walter. He had found the right line and was almost at the Shoulder, he said. The top of the Bonatti Pillar was close at hand, hallelujah!

I remember finding the last pitch of the climb desperately strenuous. With each new rope length my energy had ebbed. I felt completely done in, with a dull diesel-like throb in my head, realising that I couldn't go much further. Don kept saying that each pitch was the last – the very last and definitely the last. At least he kept me moving. Lines from Hassan ran through my mind – 'Always a little further: it may be / Beyond that last blue mountain barred with snow.'

Not that the ultimate pitch was particularly hard. I simply seemed to have used up all my steam.

During the day we hadn't noticed that the weather was getting progressively worse. Now leaden clouds were seeping in from the south and the wind had a razor's edge to it. It didn't need a prophet to tell us that we were in for bad weather.

The snow started to fall steadily and heavily and soon everything was blotted out. I remember seeing the Grandes Jorasses being swallowed in a white froth of cloud. We bivouacked on the broken rocks close to the summit. Don knew the route over the top of the mountain, but he felt that this would be too dangerous in the present weather. Walter, on the other hand, had gone down directly from where we were when he completed the West Face route the previous year, and felt that he could find the way. But not today, or rather that evening, for it was essential to get into our bivouac sacks to avoid being frozen. In ten minutes we were tied to our pegs, tethered like cowed dogs.

It was an even worse bivvy than the previous night: bitterly cold, and the fine driven snow seemed to find every cranny and tear in our bags so that we were first soaked, then frozen as if set in casting resin. Our only food was one packet of soup divided by six. There was not a great deal to be cheerful about; no joy in having climbed the route, only a numbed realisation that we had got up, but what was now much more important was to get down, and fast, for we knew that we couldn't survive long in such conditions.

We witnessed dawn through storm clouds. It was still snowing and everything was plastered: a world of white and metallic-looking ice. The ropes were again frozen solid and our plastic bivvy bags, now the worse for wear, cracked like celluloid when we tried to fold them.

Walter led the descent of the West Face, abseiling into a white nothingness on slippery ropes. The wind was so strong now that we could barely communicate. We had gone down about four rope lengths when Don, who had an acute instinct for danger, called a halt.

'Walter,' he shouted, 'I think you're wrong. This is too dicey for the descent route.' Indeed it was becoming desperately steep.

The Austrians, snow-covered figures on a minuscule ledge, were another rope length down.

'I think you are correct, Don. We will try further to the right.'

But they had trouble joining us again, and when they came alongside I could see that Richard was in a bad way, suffering from exhaustion and exposure. Don and Chris had already set off on the proper descent line.

Now, for some strange reason I was feeling stronger, possibly because I was descending, which required less effort, and I was probably more used to these abominable conditions with my Scottish background of blizzard and flood than our Austrian friends.

I tried to help Richard as best I could, while Paul and Walter were preparing the abseil belays. Walter had fallen when coming up from the low point of his descent and appeared in a nervous state. Now he launched himself on the next abseil. I could see, as if in slow motion, what was about to happen but my brain wasn't working fast enough to prevent it. He had looped a sling round a sharp spike of rock so that there was no slack, and his abseil rope was threaded through this so that when he put his weight on the doubled rope the tight sling was under great strain. It snapped when he was a few feet down, but luckily Richard, who had him on a top rope, prevented a very nasty accident.

I heard a call from Don below. 'The Flammes de Pierre, Chris. We're on the right route now.'

I breathed a sigh of relief. With my revival I could now grasp the seriousness of our situation, but in fact the worst was behind us. Both Walter and Richard, who had got into such a

had to give up due to threatening weather and lack of water. When they returned to continue their assault, instead of going back up by their own ascent line, they took the North Face route to the point where their high point was within a hundred feet. This was frightening territory: blank, featureless rock falling sheer for some 2000 feet above the base of the couloir. The only possible way to cross this smooth wall was by drilling the rock and inserting expansion bolts. The bolts are still there today, and have provided a providential escape route for climbers trapped on the West Face in bad weather.

Hermann Schriddel and Heinz Ramisch lacked both the experience and the ability to take advantage of this escape route when they joined forces with more enthusiasm than good sense to attempt the West Face in 1966. It was hardly the sort of climb on which to discover the limits of a new climbing partner, and they compounded their folly by failing to realise that the upper part of the mountain was sheathed in ice, something that was obvious even from Chamonix.

Hermann Schriddel, thirty-two, was a motor mechanic from Hanover. He was fit and experienced, though the West Face was by far the most serious climb he had ever contemplated. Heinz Ramisch was a twenty-three-year-old student from Karlsruhe who had recently completed the South Face of the Aiguille du Midi, the peak overlooking Chamonix up which the famous Mont Blanc cable car runs. The fact that this climb had taken him about eleven hours when it is often done in three should have acted as a deterrent to him, for in 1966 the West Face of the Dru was a very serious undertaking.

They bivouacked as others before them, under the rock at the Rognon de Dru, had an early start and crossed the bergschrund in the couloir at 1.00 a.m. Their progress was slow and they must have had some trouble in climbing the slabs and terraces which form the initial part of the climb. Here the rock is loose and great care must be exercised.

Fortunately the weather was fine. Conditions, at least low on the face, were good, but when they decided to bivvy for the night they had only reached 10,700 feet (3260 metres). Next day the weather still held but they were now involved with a different league of difficulty. Hermann had a thirty-foot fall, but didn't injure himself. The weather was beginning to break, with a build-up of cloud to the south. Once again they decided to bivouac, for the day was well advanced. They had only ascended 350 feet and were now at the bottom of the 295-foot dièdre, one of the great features of the climb. It started to snow.

It was a cold night and their bivouac gear left much to be desired, a duvet jacket each, a simple two-man bivvy bag and waterproof anoraks. The next day the gods smiled on them but perhaps it was a somewhat ironical smile, for had the weather continued bad they would probably have decided to retreat and they could have done so without too much difficulty, but with blue skies they decided to press on. From where they were they couldn't see the top of the face, which was plastered in ice.

Hermann had his second fall when a piton came out, but Heinz held him, burning and cutting his hands in the process. It took them all day to get to the top of the dièdre. They were both shattered and one wishes they had considered the escape route across the face on the expansion bolts to the North Face. The first bolt was only a few feet above them. However, they decided to bivvy on a minute ledge, which they knew from their route description was out of sight round a bulge. To get to this they had to do a tension traverse across a blank and vertical wall. A fixed rope hangs here and once down and across the slab, there is no way back except by climbing the rope, which is very strenuous and extremely exposed. Once over, they had really crossed their Rubicon.

With the closing of the day – 16 August – the cloud clamped in and their third bivouac on the wall was not a pleasant one, for their duvet jackets were now soaked, and they couldn't lie down on the ledge as it was minute.

In a dawn of hanging cloud, they made a right traverse on very exposed rock which took them to the base of a 100-foot crack, wide and very difficult. From this pitch there is a sheer fall for over 2000 feet to the couloir and it is very intimidating. Hermann encountered ice at the top of this section.

At last the penny dropped and the two Germans realised that they were in serious trouble. Once up the next pitch, a crack which snakes up through the overhangs, they had verified what they already knew. The climb above was impossible for them. Fighting one's way up ice-plastered vertical rock requires skill of a high order. That skill they didn't have. With their tails metaphorically between their legs they retreated to the tiny ledge on the wrong side of the tension traverse. They were exhausted.

Their friends back in Chamonix, who had been monitoring their progress through gaps in the cloud, were a little concerned when Hermann and Heinz retreated from the overhangs and came to a prolonged halt on that tiny platform, and as soon as they got a prearranged signal from the climbers that they needed help they informed the rescue service. Hermann and Heinz settled into their eyrie, little knowing that they were going to be there for seven days. To make matters worse Heinz had developed a sore throat and couldn't swallow, while Hermann was in pain with bruised ribs, a legacy of his falls.

With threatening weather, it was decided that a helicopter reconnaissance should be made, for it was assumed that one of them at least must be injured as they hadn't moved. Though the chopper managed to hover quite close to the pair it was impossible for the crew to ascertain if the climbers were hurt.

Next day, Thursday 18 August, Colonel André Gonnet, Commanding Officer of the Ecole Militaire de Haute Montagne (EMHM), deployed a team of forty alpine troops and guides who reached the Charpoua Hut by midday. He had decided to implement the rescue from above using wire rope to get to the two Germans, a distance of 1000 feet from the top position, 500 feet down the North Face and 500 feet down the West Face, a formidable undertaking. There were others who did not agree with this strategy and they, too, would soon be swinging into action independently. In the meantime, the troops kept advancing up the South Face route, the *voie normale*, to reach their objective, the Quartz Ledge, which is a couple of rope lengths short of the summit. Here there is a hole through the peak running north and south. Others had stopped en route at prearranged spots, so that a human link could be maintained up this route to expedite the movement of equipment, but there was a great deal of snow above 11,000 feet and this hampered their progress. A further hazard to the

Alpine troops was electrical discharges, and several of them suffered burns.

It is normal for the media to swing into action in the wake of a big rescue operation. This case was no exception, and as the West Face of the Dru was one of the most formidable climbs in the Alps, the rescue was obviously going to provide good copy for several days. *Paris Match*, never regarded as sluggish when there is a tragedy in the offing, gave a wide spread to a photograph of the rescue helicopter hovering close to the two Germans huddled on the tiny ledge on that unique expanse of verticality.

Two climbers, one American and one French, were independently worried about the plight of Hermann and Heinz and both decided to do something about it. René Demaison is a French guide with a long history of first ascents, who accurately describes himself as a maverick. Certainly his next adventure, rescuing Hermann and Heinz, was going to add to the controversy connected with him and lead to him being banned from the Company of Chamonix Guides.

On that Thursday afternoon, Gary Hemming was sipping coffee in a Courmayeur café, just across the Italian border from Chamonix, when he picked up a copy of *Dauphiné Libéré* and read an account of the plight of the two Germans. He knew the West Face well. In fact, with fellow American Royal Robbins, he had made the first ascent of the American Direct, a line right up the face from the Dru Glacier which avoids going into the deadly couloir. It was an impressive climb. Gary turned to his German companion, Lothar Mauch, and asked if he wanted to come with him to try to rescue Hermann and Heinz by climbing the West Face from the bottom. Lothar was more than willing, so without even finishing their coffee, they set off for Chamonix.

I think perhaps I should say a few words about Gary, who was a bit of a cult figure at the time. Gareth Hemming was born in Pasadena, California in 1933 and, after finding life at San Diego State College boring, he hot-footed it to France, where he began studying philosophy, that subject which can camouflage other motives and interests so effectively. Like many American climbers of that generation, he lived on a shoestring budget, a mere five dollars a week which his mother sent him, and acquired comprehensive bivouac training, as he slept under the Seine bridges for several winters and generally bummed around. His summer retreat was usually Chamonix where he was easily recognised by his thick long blond hair and six-foot six-inch height. In fact there is an account of a journalist asking him how tall he was and Gary telling him that way back he was only six foot four inches, but during internment by the Japanese in the Pacific war he was stretched as a punishment. After the reporter had dutifully taken note Gary said to him, 'No, I'm kidding, I was actually this height at birth.'

He had remarkable looks and a serene expression, yet beneath it I don't think he had found the elusive Nirvana he was looking for. I met him several times and one couldn't help being impressed by the man, both as an individual and as a climber. With his thick red pullover and the coloured patches on his trousers he reminded me of an impecunious knight errant.

In Chamonix, Gary called to see Colonel Gonnet and volunteered his services. He had met the colonel before, but in somewhat strained circumstances. Gary had been nominated to attend a special training course for talented climbers at the prestigious Ecole Nationale, but the long-haired American was refused admission unless he got a haircut and removed his beard; Gary did neither, so he didn't get on the course. However, the colonel wasn't one to bear grudges. He supplied the tall American with a walkie-talkie and other equipment and wished him 'bonne chance'.

After enquiring at a climbing shop as to which top-ranking alpinists were in town, Gary tracked them down and enlisted their help. There was a German called Gehrad, two leading French climbers, François Guillot and Gilles Bodin, and lastly, a friend of mine, Mick Burke. Mick had been on the West Face before, but was forced back from the ninety-metre dièdre, one of the crux pitches, in nasty weather and with an injured companion. They had abseiled right down Gary's route, the American Direct, a feat which Hermann and Heinz could have done had they been prudent enough. Mick was always willing to help a climber in need and I was later to respect him for this on an attempt to find a colleague who had been buried under séracs in the Everest Icefall.

While the military operation was being consolidated on the Quartz Ledge, high above in atrocious conditions, Gary's party set off up the couloir at 10.00 a.m. on 19 August. It was about 2.00 p.m. when they traversed left over a section known as the grey slabs. The weather was deteriorating and they prepared to bivouac on rock ledges there. Over a thousand feet above, Hermann and Heinz resigned themselves to another freezing night. Yet despite their prolonged incarceration, on their prison with one wall, they never lost hope and knew that they would be rescued.

Meanwhile, René Demaison had also taken things into his own hands and landed by helicopter with his friend Vincent Mercie on the Dru Glacier. He had earlier volunteered his services to the Guides Bureau but had been told that the bureau hadn't been consulted or asked to help, so they rather huffily hadn't called out any of the guides.

Though conditions were desperate on the summit, it wasn't exactly a picnic for those at the bottom of the face either. Cloud had a tenacious grip on the Dru and it was raining at the bottom of the couloir. Stones and rocks came whistling past, intent on destruction. Undeterred by these missiles, René and Vincent climbed quickly, using a 160-foot-long climbing rope. Higher up, the couloir narrows in a bottleneck and stonefall was so concentrated here that they realised they would never get through unscathed, so reluctantly decided to bivvy for the night. Rain turned to snow then back to rain again and a soggy mist made the gully an eerie place, but the ledge which they had found was reasonably missile-free even though it lacked creature comforts. At least they felt that in the cold of dawn the narrows of the gully would be safer with the rock debris above frozen in place, until the temperature rose.

That day, Gary's party had seen the chopper coming in and later spied the two figures making their way up the couloir. Everybody on the mountain had had a miserable night, possibly those lower down suffering the worst.

On 20 August the weather hadn't improved. Visibility wasn't even the length of the climbing ropes. René and Vincent ran the gauntlet of the couloir narrows and they could see Gary's party, only a hundred feet above them on the ledges where they had lodged for the night. To speed their progress over verglased rock, Gehrad, one of the Germans, dropped René a rope. With the addition of the two Frenchmen, the rescue party was now up to eight. It was 9.00 a.m., and Gary had perhaps optimistically said that they could reach the two trapped Germans in a day. That might have been possible on dry rock, but conditions were abysmal and not going to improve. René thought they were moving too slowly so they agreed to have the fastest climbers out front: Gary and François Guillot, followed by René and Vincent. The others were to follow, carrying the bulk of the equipment, and caching some of it on the ledges.

So while René and Vincent got a brew going, Gary and François set off. But Gary went off route. Though he had done the much harder American Direct to the left, he hadn't in fact done the lower part of the West Face route and a couple of pitches up René and Vincent caught them up. Gary's error was soon corrected and he carried on, leading towards the Fissure Vignes, one of the hard sections of the climb.

About this time, 12.00 noon, down in Chamonix another decision was taken. The Ecole Nationale and the Guides Bureau agreed to send a group of top guides and instructors up the North Face of the Dru to try to reach Hermann and Heinz from that side. Now the Germans were being approached by every possible way. The media were having a banquet of drama and they made the most of it with national television coverage and international press saturation. As always in such situations, there are individuals willing to crawl out of the woodwork to pass supercilious judgment, and René fell victim to a great deal of this by his act in pre-empting what in fact his organisation, the Guides Bureau, did later.

The North Face party had one of the most dangerous approaches, for they were in direct line of fire from above, where ledges were being excavated in the snow and belays installed. All debris from these operations came right down their route.

The group climbing the West Face weren't now subjected to objective danger – the huge overhangs above ensured that, but it was still unpleasant and difficult climbing, with icy water running down their sleeves. Even so Gary was laid back and expounded his philosophy of life to an exasperated François.

Higher up on a pitch called the Forty Metre Wall, René had a twenty-foot fall when a peg came out, but he was unhurt. The rock on this section is so steep that he fell clear, but it must have been disturbing to peel with such a dramatic backdrop and only air below, for 1800 feet.

It was dusk by the time Gary had ascended the Jammed Block pitch. This derives its name from a huge chockstone jammed into a very steep chimney. The boulder effectively blocks the chimney and has to be climbed by a thirty-foot overhang. Needless to say the scalp of this huge rock holds snow, as the sun doesn't reach it. But as temperature rises during the day some does melt and with a night frost, ice forms, sometimes in quantity. That evening it was meltwater which was cascading down, directly on top of the climbers so that they were soaked to the skin. They settled down for the next bivouac there – another uncomfortable night. It was 11.00 p.m. They shouted up to the two Germans, who they knew were now quite close, but there was no reply.

That day the weather had been so severe on the summit that virtually nothing was done. The helicopter which was scheduled to transport the winch to the Quartz Ledge party couldn't fly.

The Hemming/Demaison party still had 300 feet to go to reach the Germans, but this involved some very hard climbing. Above was the ninety-metre dièdre. It was now 21 August and Gary started up at 6.00 a.m. with François. The cloud had cleared and they hoped their luck was going to change. Alas, this wasn't to be. René and Vincent delayed their departure from the Jammed Block to organise equipment ready to assist the Germans back across the pendulum pitch. Meantime, down below, Mick Burke and the others were busy hauling up ropes and equipment for the abseil down the face.

By the time René and Vincent had climbed the dièdre, Gary was moving across the pendulum pitch. He was now very close to Hermann and Heinz. He shouted to them, 'I'm coming.' They replied but their call was unintelligible. In a few minutes Gary had reached their ledge, followed quickly by François. It was midday.

57

Hermann offered Gary a nut. For six days they had been on a starvation ration. Gary dryly mentioned to Demaison when he arrived that had the Germans been French they would have gobbled all their nuts on the first day.

One is tempted to compare this rescue to spiders converging on a pair of flies. Just at this moment the two separate ropes from the North Face gained a ledge not more than a hundred feet away and slightly higher. Yves Pollet-Villard was in charge of this group and he had direct radio contact with Chamonix. Now developed a discourse on how to dispose of the prey. Yves, as representing the establishment and the official rescue party, was all for taking the two uninjured Germans down the North Face. René pointed out that this route was too strenuous for the weak and shattered climbers, and Gary, who had been the first to reach the Germans, was given the casting vote. He advocated abseiling down the West Face. In the meantime, high above, Wolfgang Egle, a young German friend of Hermann and Heinz, somehow got snarled up in his rope while abseiling and was strangled.

The Germans were given dry warm clothing and after they had been fitted with safety harnesses the long descent began. Gary and François set off and did two 130-foot abseils down to the Jammed Block. Vincent then abseiled one rope length and waited at a stance. René sent down Hermann, abseiling with a safety rope on. It was an incredibly exposed situation, but he managed it. Vincent untied him once he had reached his minute ledge and prepared him for the next stage down to the base of the dièdre. Meanwhile René was busy sending Heinz down.

Below they met up with the rest of Gary's party and all decided to bivouac as it was 4.00 p.m. There were now ten of them occupying the bivvy ledge. For a cushion they had snow, which melted underneath them. They were all saturated and shivering. But they were soon to forget that particular misery as an electrical storm of unusual violence lit the Aiguille in a blaze of light, racking them all with violent body-arching shocks. They were desperate to escape from this charged and sulphurous hell, but there was nowhere to go. They were effectively chained to the rock by their karabiners. To unclip would have been instant suicide. The fact that there were bunches of metal pitons about didn't help matters. Gilles Bodin, who was sitting on a pile of these pegs, as a 'damp course' in his personal pool of water, had a series of shocks through sensitive regions. René Demaison was the worst affected: his face was swollen, and he had trouble breathing. Hermann and Heinz, who were beneath an overhang, had a reasonable night. It is interesting to note how these two young men withstood the strain of their prolonged stay on the face. The fact that they had always been confident that they would be rescued must have played a part in their ultimate survival. There is nothing worse than giving up hope of rescue. It seems that if you give up hope, hope gives up you. Another danger for the rescued is the tendency to relinquish the struggle once the rescuers arrive, when in many cases the casualty still has to display determination to win through and get off the mountain.

At 5.00 a.m. they were up to a fresh snow cover and at 6.00 a.m. they were off. Over the walkie-talkie they heard that the weather was to improve. Mick and Gary started abseiling first. It was their intention to establish a continuous line of rope for almost a thousand feet. While the Germans were being safeguarded on their abseils, the ropes above were retrieved and passed down to Mick and Gary. Hermann and Heinz now made up for their slow ascent for they were expedited down that intimidating face at high speed to a heroes' welcome.

Gary was the man of the hour and the press latched on to him as if he were the principal character in the crucifixion. The two Germans were taken to hospital, but there was little wrong with them. Their friend, Wolfgang Egle, still hung from his rope at the top of the mountain and would be taken down to rest as soon as the weather improved.

The inevitable rescue post mortem got under way in the press. It had been one of the biggest operations of its kind, with many alpine troops, guides and climbers risking their lives to help. In fact Hermann and Heinz could possibly have been reached and evacuated by any of the routes employed and the way they had been taken down had proved entirely viable.

Gary continued his nomadic life in the high Alps, but now he was recognised everywhere he went. In 1966 he earned some money clearing the roofs of tall buildings in Chamonix after winter snow, and when spring came round he set off for Alaska, still outwardly his normal carefree self, taking the handout of life as it came. He returned to the United States and on 6 August 1969, just over three years after the Dru rescue, he was found shot dead in the Grand Teton National Park in Wyoming. It was accepted that he had committed suicide. Why he returned to the stately Tetons to die no one will ever know.

Mick Burke and I went on two later expeditions to Everest's South-West Face. On the second of these, in 1975, Mick disappeared when close to the summit. It is very possible he had reached it first.

Plucked from the Pillar

Such is its reputation for mountain accidents that even in the short time since Emmanuel Schmutz sent me this account there has been an alarming increase in climbing accidents in the Chamonix Alps. Emmanuel has taken part in many evacuations in these mountains and, typically of a climber and guide who has to deal with high drama as a daily routine, this tale stands as a memorial to understatement. It is difficult to imagine a more impressive location to enact a rescue. It was completed competently by true professionals.

EMMANUEL SCHMUTZ
Nearly fifty per cent of all mountain rescues in France take place in the Mont Blanc massif. The number of incidents increased from about twenty-four a year in 1959 to an average of over three hundred in the 1980s, a frightening escalation in twenty years. In the five-year period up to 1985, 245 climbers have been killed in the Mont Blanc area and over a thousand badly injured. Two-thirds of the accidents occur in July and

August when there can be more than two thousand climbers a
day on the mountains.

Mountain rescue for the Mont Blanc massif at Chamonix is
now based on a specialised unit, the PGHM (Peleton de
Gendarmerie de Haute Montagne), about forty strong, most
of them guides or aspirant guides. Before, it was the province
of the guides of the Chamonix Company, but by 1958 the
number of accidents in this overcrowded part of the Alps
made people realise it was essential to create an organisation
whose sole purpose was mountain rescue. The need for a force
like the PGHM was driven home by the tragic accident on
Mont Blanc at the end of December 1956. It was obvious on
this rescue that the set-up was totally inadequate.

Various other interests were later incorporated within the
structure of the PGHM, the army (EMHM: Ecole Militaire de
Haute Montagne), the Ecole Nationale de Ski et d'Alpinisme
(ENSA) and the Company of Guides, which provides a
back-up to the PGHM.

At present two Alouette III helicopters which can carry
seven people are available. These two machines are owned by
the Gendarmerie and the Civil Security and stay in the
Chamonix valley during the peak summer period. Their
off-mountain duties include the evacuation of road accident
casualties and general hospital ambulance duties.

The present policy is to use these helicopters for ninety per
cent of mountain rescue situations, which is now possible due
to their more powerful turbines and sophisticated winches,
able to control a fifty-metre cable.

On a busy day there can be ten rescues; without helicopters
it would be impossible, as most of the evacuations are difficult
and dangerous, both to patient and rescuer.

In ideal conditions, using the Alouettes, an injured person
can be delivered to the Chamonix hospital in as little as ten
minutes after the accident. In the past, it would have taken one
or even several days, involving dozens of rescuers.

Previously, the guides coming back home exhausted from a
rescue had sometimes to set out again the next day. Now, as in
other parts of the world, the helicopters have taken much of
the drudgery out of the job.

The detail of some tragic rescue is often vividly retained in the rescuer's memory, though the media reports may make little of the tragedy. A major effort on the part of a skilled rescue team may be only a few lines amongst the news items: 'The mountain strikes again: Two deaths in the Goûter Couloir . . .' leaving readers indifferent to the suffering of those concerned. For bad news is good news as far as selling papers is concerned.

That's why I've chosen to tell a happy story: a tale of two young people, not really aware of the dangers in the mountains, but fortunately everything turned out well in the end. It could so easily have been a tragedy.

On Saturday 19 June 1976, Paul Vincendon and Didier Hendry set off to climb the South-West Pillar of the Dru. Though it wasn't what they expected, they profited in experience and went forward to maturity. It was the kind of character-building adventure which is said to be so beneficial when you are in your late teens.

Paul and Didier bivouacked in the open at the Rognon de Dru, ready for an early start in the morning. The Rognon de Dru is a wonderful place; one feels overwhelmed by the sheer scale of the West Face above. In daylight, if you're lucky, you can spot climbers like coloured dots, seven or eight hundred metres higher, perhaps at grips with the difficulties of the American Direct, the West Face or the Bonatti Pillar. At night it is certainly one of the most beautiful 'bedrooms' an alpinist can imagine. This cathedral of the Mont Blanc massif has attracted millions of people, both climbers and tourists, thanks to the cog railway from Chamonix to Montenvers, the station across the Mer de Glace. From there, with the aid of telescopes, they can fight, slip, sweat, or Walter Mitty-like, believe they are the heroes of an unfair struggle with the smooth and vertical rock of this giant above them.

In the morning our two young men prepared to tackle the first difficulties. Before leaving the valley they had sensibly given their schedule to the OHM (Office de la Haute Montagne), as well as an intended return date from the climb. The OHM was the brainchild of the late Gerard Devoursoux. It supplies information on snow conditions and weather, and also informs the PGHM if a party is overdue.

Though the night was mild, the snow grated under the

boys' crampons, indicating that it was freezing. At 5.00 a.m.
they crossed the rimaye with the aid of an étrier. They were
making fast time. The Dru Couloir, which angles steeply up
the bottom of the West Face, is a death trap down which
rockfalls thunder unpredictably. Many climbers have been
killed and injured here. The Couloir is effectively blocked off
at the top end by the wall at the Flammes de Pierre. Here is the
start of the Bonatti Pillar, probably the most majestic sweep of
rock in the Alps.

It was now 10.00 a.m. Crampons and ice axes were returned
to the rucksacks, for the next few thousand feet would be rock
climbing. Paul and Didier were relieved to be out of the
'Valley of Death'. But their shoulders already ached with their
large rucksacks, even the minimum is too heavy. Both boys
had been training hard for this expedition; first at the climbing
school, then on their own, wearing climbing boots on
exacting rock routes rather than the specialised lightweight
ones favoured by climbers for hard rock problems on lower
crags. On such serious climbs as the Bonatti Pillar the axiom is
let's not get too ethical: if there is a peg in a crack you use it.
There's no one about to point an accusing finger. Time and
storms are the adversary.

If the telescope addicts were in position below they would
be thinking in headlines: 'Cheating Death by the Skin of Their
Teeth', watching them thrutching up a Grade IV athletic!
They probably wouldn't know that the IV of the Mont Blanc
massif is often harder than a Grade V in the Vercors or
Calanques.

In the Mont Blanc massif guide, the route doesn't seem
frightening when you read the description 'V, A1, A2' and so
on. There never seems to be exceptional difficulty. However,
the truth can quickly be felt in the arms, especially with the
dead weight of the rucksack hanging from your shoulders.

The two men agreed to lead alternate pitches. But after the
second one, Didier, the weaker of the two, let Paul go first. It
was soon clear to Paul that the climb was too serious for his
companion who was making heavy weather of the difficulties
and seemed to take ages.

Time was slipping by, but they didn't even eat, and in the
afternoon, the weather became overcast, more like August

than June. A violent hailstorm swept over them with devastating suddenness, followed by torrential rain. They were forced to bivouac where they were, soaked and frozen.

Making the best of a bad job they settled down for the night on a minuscule ledge. Later the clouds cleared, giving way to a cold which seemed to settle into their bone marrow. There was no hot food to eat, they had left their stove behind to save weight. Even so, they were still in high spirits; such is the temperament of mountaineers.

The stars glimmered that night, glimmered with cold. If only the sky could be overcast, Paul thought, it would be a bit warmer at least. Getting going in the morning was hard; they had had a sleepless night. And on this South-West Pillar the sun does not get round to thawing out frozen cracks and numbed muscles before the end of the morning. But the sky was now azure blue and the young men had no desire to retreat. They felt optimistic, despite the desperate night. So they pressed on, Paul still out front: he had already completed some major climbs in other parts of the Alps and was confident he could lead his friend to the summit.

Each year younger and younger climbers tackle fashionable routes, especially rock climbs such as the American Direct on the West Face of the Dru, or the Dru Couloir. Their record times are evidence of this youth revolution: North Face of the Droites, three hours; West Face of the Dru (solo), three hours ten minutes; Grand Pilier d'Angle, three hours; each year faster and faster: now the Matterhorn North Wall, the Eigerwand *and* the Grandes Jorasses in a day! Paul hadn't yet graduated to this elite band.

Immediately after leaving the bivouac Paul had to tackle a testing pitch, made worse by the cold. The crack was graded IV athletic but it was hard. Didier, when it was his turn, climbed up the rope, assisted by Paul.

An artificial pitch left them in a cold sweat. The wooden wedges inserted by earlier climbers looked as if they had been manufactured from offcuts left over from the Ark.

Paul felt sure that they must be the first party to do the route that year. It was necessary to check every piton, every wedge. In 1976 aluminium wedges or chocks weren't widely used by French climbers and they tended to use pitons whose regular insertion and removal from the cracks left permanent scars.

After climbing for some hours, the two men found themselves at the bottom of the Red Wall. All the pegs were dubious and some positively insecure, and already half a day had vanished. They swallowed some nuts for lunch.

Further up is the Austrians' Crack and Paul started a new pitch which should take him to the bottom of this fissure which goes through a small dihedral at Grade V, then up a slab. But a peg at arm's length looked unsafe. To avoid it, he decided to move right to a small overhang, then up an easy crack.

There was a good wooden wedge in this overhang. Without thinking, Paul asked for some slack rope and clipped on to it with a karabiner. He realised as he continued that he did not have enough security, retreated to the wooden wedge and then clipped to a peg just below. He then attached his étrier to it and stood up – but not for long! Suddenly he was falling, rock was passing in front of his eyes; he struck a protruding piece of it and felt a stabbing pain in both thigh and ankle. After thirty feet he stopped abruptly and swung gently to and fro, horrified to see that a strand of the rope was cut just above him by the sharp edge of the rock.

Didier, apparently more shocked than Paul, desperately pulled him in to the stance. Paul had a struggle because of his aching right ankle, also his harness was cutting into his thigh and he thought he might have broken his leg.

There was nothing more they could do that day, it was 2.00 p.m. and Paul was stiffening up. He saw a small ledge below and they succeeded in getting to this tiny sanctuary poised high above the Couloir which they had climbed, what felt to them, so long ago. Gratefully they sat down. A short time later, in the middle of the afternoon, another storm blew up. They curled up against each other to keep warm, there was nothing else they could do. Lightning flickered round the Dru in a heavenly electrical display. Repeated shocks racked their bodies. Being soaked to the skin didn't help matters either. Later the skies cleared and a biting frost enveloped the mountains. It was going to be another frigid night.

Around 7.30 p.m. they heard the throb of a helicopter coming close. Having told the OHM that they expected to be down that evening, they thought it must be coming to see if they were in difficulties. But the helicopter didn't arrive. It was on another mission.

They decided to stay where they were the following day in order to rest and in case the pilot had seen them but couldn't get close enough and would try again next day.

This night between Monday and Tuesday was as cold as the previous ones. Their food had almost run out. When dawn broke, they saw the day was fine, but the sun, as ever, took time to reach them with its warmth. They could not face another day on that lonely ledge. There was still no sign of rescue, so they decided to try to get off on their own by taking the Weber route, a traverse which would allow them to escape across to the top of the Flammes de Pierre and then on to the normal route for the Petit Dru. Paul was unsure how his injuries would fare in this ambitious last-ditch bid to get back down to the Charpoua Refuge. A further short violent storm punctuated the end of the day, in which both climbers suffered more electric shocks and were again saturated. At 7.30 p.m. they heard a helicopter once more. This time it came closer and closer and hovered in front of them. Now they knew that they hadn't been forgotten. They made the conventional signals of distress, raising both arms in a V, meaning Yes, we need help.

Because it was so late, the PGHM decided to postpone the rescue operation till the following day, Wednesday.

That evening a team of eight of the most experienced rescuers was selected, and a quantity of equipment prepared to get the two climbers off the Weber route to the Flammes de Pierre. An essential item of equipment, the Pomagalski winch, was put in a rucksack. Being both heavy and difficult to carry, it was usually the responsibility of the latest recruit.

Very early on Wednesday 23 June the rescuers were warned by the Met Office that they would have a storm during the afternoon. But when? They could only hope they would beat it back before it broke. At first light, around 5.00 a.m., the rescue team were winched from the helicopter on to a small shelf on the edge of the Flammes de Pierre, some 250 metres above and to the side of the ledge where the two climbers were.

The problem for the rescue team was not in the vertical distance but in the horizontal one between them and the climbers. It is easy to rope down or to use a cable from a point directly above an injured party. But when traverses are involved, the problems escalate. They didn't know much about Paul and Didier, or if one or even both were injured. If it were a serious injury, evacuation was going to be highly technical.

As soon as they landed, the rescuers started to fix ropes across the difficult face above the climbers. Their rucksacks were heavy and made this manoeuvre hazardous. Eventually they found a steeply angled ledge, almost directly above the boys. They were now about a hundred metres above. It was essential to find cracks from which to secure the winch to pitons. Here, however, the rock was very compact and they had to make the best of a bad lot of belays; it seemed impossible to get a good piton in. Finally around 10.00 a.m. (five hours after having been landed from the helicopter) they got the winch in place.

Even with the dodgy belays there was a volunteer ready to go down on the thin cable. It was Alan, one of the guides, who went down with a walkie-talkie. The lowering operation is fairly simple, just a matter of braking with the winch, which doesn't require much effort. After about eighty metres Alan had to make a tricky pendulum to get round a rock edge. He made it and arrived at the two climbers, who hailed him as if he were the Messiah.

Time was slipping away and they decided to winch up the three men together. Even though the winch can lift over a ton, the effort required from the rescuers was going to be considerable on the cramped and dangerous stance.

They knew that it would take the six of them nearly two hours to get the three men to their ledge. Later they were to realise that it would have been better to do it in two operations instead of one. That would involve two men at a time because you needed to keep a rescuer on the cable to prevent it penduluming. Eventually, after much sweating, they got the three men up to that uncomfortable ledge at half-past twelve.

The rescuers didn't mutter about the incompetence of the two climbers. There was only the satisfaction of having completed a difficult and dangerous job successfully.

From their lofty perch they could now see that the sky, which they had forgotten to look at, was getting darker. Another storm was almost upon them. Within a few minutes all hell broke loose, the same ingredients as the two men had experienced before. Lightning, rain and snow. They had to tie on to prevent themselves being plucked off the face.

Everybody was soaked to the skin. The sodden ropes froze into steel hawsers and the rescuers realised what Paul and Didier had been through in the earlier storms. They were lucky to have survived.

The problem now was how to get down. Just then it was out of the question to make a move. To untie from the safety ropes would have been suicidal. But if the helicopter didn't return they would have to start considering the long and laborious way down the frozen rock, towards the glacier and the Charpoua Refuge. Just when they had decided on this drastic course of action, which would mean leaving their heavy gear to be picked up later, they heard the comforting beat of the Alouette through the cloud. What a relief!

Over the radio the rescuers were told that both helicopters were hoping to pick them up. It was to be a personal challenge for the rescue pilots. The machines inched their way towards that exposed rocky outpost. The first helicopter hovered overhead. Didier and Paul were winched aboard. In minutes, they were borne from that harsh environment to the Chamonix hospital. The second helicopter managed to get a skid on to the granite edge of the rock and eventually all the team were taken off. Paul fortunately had only sustained severe bruising and was shortly to be climbing again.

That night, the rescuers met in a restaurant to celebrate the success of the operation. They felt it was a call-out of considerable technical difficulty which doesn't happen too often these days, and what was even more important it had a happy ending.

4

SNOW ON THE EQUATOR

This tale of a rescue on Mount Kenya is one of the most amazing in the annals of mountaineering. The rescuers had not only to combat the technical difficulties of the climb, but some had also to deal with the debilitating effect of altitude sickness. One rescuer was killed. The man they were trying to reach they expected to be already dead from his injuries. Several of the main characters in this high African adventure still feel, after seventeen years, that it was the most demanding and profound period of their lives.

Robert Chambers of the Mountain Club of Kenya was in charge of the rescue bid and he can still recall every detail of those days in 1970. Two friends of mine took part in the operation. Dr Oswald Oelz was one of the two Austrian climbers involved in the accident, it was his colleague who fell. John Temple was one of the rescuers who made a great contribution, especially in the early stages of the rescue. My recollections of John Temple are associated with balmy days in the Cuillins of Skye, warm rock and lumps of uncompromising commercial glucose as hard as gabbro, which caused temporary discomfort to my stomach and permanent damage to my teeth. John had an inexhaustible source of glucose, and Ian Clough, who was the third member of this happy rock-climbing trio, swore that the lumps would make excellent artificial chockstones from which to attach running belays. This was back in 1958 and the alloy chock had still to be invented. We enjoyed many routes together during that summer before John Temple left for Nairobi where he did some impressive climbs on Mount Kenya, some of them first ascents.

The first European to record seeing what later became known as Mount Kenya was a resolute German missionary,

Dr Johann Krapf, who looked northwards from a village in the Wa–Kamba district on 3 December 1849 and saw 'snow on the equator'. 'It appeared to me,' he wrote, 'like a gigantic wall, on whose summit I observed two immense towers, or horns, as you might call them. These horns or towers, which are at a short distance from each other, give the mountain a grand and majestic appearance which raised in my mind overwhelming feelings.' Though natives had spoken earlier of the mountain to explorers and missionaries, they were not believed, nor immediately was Dr Krapf. Indeed it was to be fifty years before someone climbed the mountain which gave the state its name.

The first recorded attempt was made in 1893 by Professor Gregory, whose loyal Zanzibari bearers made better porters than climbers and had an understandable distrust of snow and ice. One agreed to rope up with his master, but when a hold broke under him his nerve broke too and he addressed the professor: 'That is all very well for Wajuuxi [lizards] and Wazungu [white men] but Zanzibaris can't do that!'

So the first ascent fell to the explorer Sir Halford Mackinder who six years later climbed Batian (17,085 feet/5199 metres), the higher of the twin summits, accompanied, as was the fashion of those gentlemanly days, by two Courmayeur guides, César Ollier and Joseph Brocherel. The second summit, Nelion (17,022 feet/5186 metres) was not defeated until Eric Shipton and Percy Wynn Harris climbed it in 1929.

Today the mountain and its satellites are within the Mount Kenya National Park. The plateau of moorland surrounding the peaks above 11,000 feet (3351 metres) could be from the pages of *Lord of the Rings*. Giant heather and groundsel grow like twenty-foot trees, while the lobelia stands as tall as a man, and below, the forest teems with a Noah's Ark of fauna, from rhino to leopard, who sometimes trespass on to this moorland.

The twin peaks soar in splendid volcanic isolation over the East African savannah and while the area is a magnet for tourists and climbers, the ascent of Mount Kenya is by no means easy.

The two young Austrian doctors felt justly proud when they reached the summit of Batian by the hard North Face on

70

5 September 1970. I first met Dr Oswald Oelz two years later at the Yak and Yeti Hotel in Kathmandu when he was a member of an Austrian Manaslu Expedition. This is the start of Oswald Oelz's account of their amazing experience. After him various members of the rescue team contribute their own memories of an operation unparalleled on the mountains of Africa.

DR OSWALD OELZ

On 5 September at 1.30 p.m. my friend, twenty-nine-year-old Dr Gerd Judmaier, and I reached the main summit of Mount Kenya, known as Batian. This was our first trip outside the Alps and we were ecstatic to have reached our goal. We left the Kami Hut at 5.30 a.m. and found the climbing enjoyable, but difficult in places, due to ice in the chimneys. It was the first ascent from the Kami Hut that season.

We stayed on the summit for a few minutes only since we were entirely in cloud and it had started to snow. To gain the descent point we traversed three pitches of the summit ridge to Shipton's Notch where I found two old abseil slings around a rock but used a new one to ensure a safe rappel down the face. Shipton's Notch is a comfortable place on the ridge and has enough space for several people to stand there. We were still roped up, Gerd was standing one metre to my left looking down the face and was holding on to a big rock block with his right hand. While fixing the abseil sling I suddenly to my horror saw the block breaking away and falling down the face together with Gerd. They both vanished. Somehow I managed to get the rapidly disappearing rope into my hands and tried to arrest the fall. My hands and fingers were burned immediately. But suddenly the rope snagged for an instant, interrupting Gerd's fall as he crashed diagonally down the face after a twelve-metre plunge. This enabled me to take a turn of the rope round my arm to stop him.

Immediately I heard him crying to give him some slack. I let him down another two or three metres. Writing this after all these years I still don't know how I managed to hold him.

He shouted up to me that he had an open fracture of his right leg. I quickly rappeled to where he lay, noting en route that our rope was severely damaged in several places by the rock fall.

Gerd was lying on steep loose rock on a ledge, and was bleeding from various head injuries, having lost his helmet in the fall. More serious, however, was the condition of his right leg where the tibia was sticking out of his stocking just above the climbing boot and a ten-centimetre splinter from the distal part of his tibia was lying quite separately beside him. This injury was bleeding severely. He had apparently also damaged the left leg. I applied a strong tourniquet around his right thigh and thereby controlled the bleeding.

Gerd was entirely realistic about his prospects for the immediate future: he calmly discussed three options for dying:

Shock and bleeding.

Freezing to death.

Fat embolism originating from his open bone.

Neither of us saw much hope in getting him down in time to obtain the vital medication.

He thought that his chances of survival were only a few per cent. I thought, but kept it to myself, that he didn't have any chance whatsoever. But we both resolved to fight, to fight as we'd never fought before.

I wrapped all our clothes around him and covered him completely with a bivouac sack. I also left our food supply, which was limited to 250 c.c. of whisky and one can of fruit. He asked me to say goodbye to everybody and said, 'You know I had a good life.' I told him not to give up, that I would get help in time, and I left hardly able to control my grief and tears.

I had to tie what was left of the rope together at several points so that I could now only rappel a maximum of ten metres on the descent. It was snowing heavily and I was full of remorse, knowing for certain that I would not find him alive when I came back.

It was almost dark when I arrived at the Kami Hut. There were eight British and American climbers there and when I told them of the accident they immediately offered to help. The strongest of them, a Zambian British expatriate called Bert Burrage, climbed in the dark for two and a half hours to the Top Hut at 15,700 feet where there was emergency first aid and a solar-powered radio. He got through to the police at Naro Moru, a village at the base of the mountain, and a rescue operation was then set in motion.

In 1970 the procedure for dealing with a major rescue on Mount Kenya was hypothetical, for until that year there had been no call for a serious evacuation from the virtual summit of the mountain.

Robert Chambers and fellow members of the Mountain Club of Kenya had speculated about such an emergency, and when it came to pass, like so many dedicated mountaineers, they did their damnedest to save human life and in so doing risked their own. Robert describes the situation and the events leading up to a spectacular rescue.

ROBERT CHAMBERS

In the Mountain Club of Kenya (MCK) in 1970, no one would have called our mountain rescue team strong. The club had perhaps a dozen people who could lead Severe or harder, and a dozen more with enough mountaineering and rock climbing experience to be of some use. We also had a few contacts in Uganda and Tanzania who were outside possibilities for help in a long rescue. Many of our members were expatriates on short-term contracts, which made it difficult to build up a team, or even to agree on and practise standard procedures. Every few months we would grit our teeth and force ourselves to devote the better part of a Sunday to a rather hazardous practice, usually at Leukenia, the most popular and accessible rocks near Nairobi, and actually owned by the club. After these practices, with their terrifying lowers of sporting victims, and their lively discussions about methods and procedures, I always heaved a sigh of relief that nothing worse had happened than the loss of climbing time. Our equipment was a mixture of the basic, two stretchers, and the avant garde, a cacolet (rescue litter), plus two 100-metre drums of wire for direct lowers. Every now and then we had call-outs on Mount Kenya, but usually for pulmonary oedema. The only really big climbing rescue before 1970 was not a true test of the MCK rescue team, because eight fit Germans happened to be already on the mountain and they did most of the climbing involved. Also the weather was good. We had never had to do a major rescue at altitude on our own. The one mock rescue we attempted on Mount Kenya was a dreadful thing. Many of the 'rescuers' were more or less useless from mountain sickness.

Even less confidence was inspired by our 'dry' rescues in the clubhouse. These were exercises in logistical fantasy, like military TEWTs (Tactical Exercises Without Troops). We would imagine an accident and then follow through our guesses of what might happen, hour by hour and day by day. No amount of beer made these anything but sobering occasions. Once we picked a really difficult place. We took one of the most inaccessible places on the mountain – Shipton's Notch on the West Ridge, just below the summit of Batian. This we reckoned would be harder than anywhere on the normal route. By the end of the evening, having allowed for mountain sickness and other contingencies, we could see no way the rescue could be completed. Hardly anyone could even reach the place. Despite the support of the Kenya Police and the Mountain National Parks, there was no way we could think to get someone off Shipton's Notch dead, let alone alive.

I used to daydream about mountain rescue. It added an edge to life to know you might be called out any moment for some dramatic excitement, and it was an exhilarating fantasy world to enter, with plenty of scope for seeing oneself in a heroic role. As long as it did not really happen. We had procedures and did practices, but we didn't have experience.

Jenny and I were lying in bed at home in Nairobi after a rather good Saturday evening and just dropping off into the deep and blissful, when the phone rang. There are moments for telephone calls, and this was not one of them. So I had to make the drowsy joke, 'It's a rescue!' The phone crackled and a voice said, 'This is Naro Moru Police Station . . .'

As convenor of the MCK Mountain Rescue Sub-Committee, I was automatically in charge of the climbing part of the rescue. Jenny and I telephoned around but could raise no other member of the climbing team, so we left the task to the Kenya Police Headquarters. I spoke to Bill Woodley, the Warden of the Mountain National Parks and a highly skilled pilot, and arranged to meet him at the Naro Moru airstrip at dawn. We then went to the Mountain Club, collected medicines and jammed the cacolet with difficulty into our

Volkswagen Beetle. It left little room. I curled up as best I could to try to sleep while Jenny, pregnant with our first child, drove through the night, the 120-odd miles to Naro Moru.

The first question was whether the climber was still alive. After a night alone with a broken leg at that altitude, he might well not be. So we flew up to see, and also to recce a rescue route. We took off in the little two-seater just after dawn. It was one of those Kenya mornings so clear it almost hurts. We climbed slowly up over the forest, and then the moorland, and then finally breasted a col and ridge to the North Face and the summit. And there we could see a red blob on a ledge just below Shipton's Notch. And the blob waved. We flew right past and could see him well, lying there waving vigorously. I think that having seen Gerd Judmaier, as a person, alive on that ledge, was crucial for me in the days that followed.

As we flew round, I had a good look at his position. There were two possible rescue lines. One was along the summit ridge and down the North Ridge by the Firmin-Hicks route. The carry along the ridge looked to me out of the question, given our few climbers and the possibility of altitude sickness. And it was difficult to imagine our ever being able to complete the rescue down the long North Ridge which followed. Also any rescue along that line would take so long that Judmaier would be dead long before we got him off. So I looked at the alternative, so appealing from the air – a direct lower down the North Face, in two stages. It would need either our two drums of wire or perhaps two hundred metres of rope, but it looked feasible. If we could get the rope or wire, and the light cacolet to the Notch, plus three or four climbers, we would stand a chance of getting him down and off quickly. Or so it seemed to me, looking at it from the plane.

We landed back in Naro Moru. A few climbers were beginning to arrive. Judmaier's companion, Oswald Oelz, was also a doctor, and we got the message that the top priority was plasma to restore Judmaier's body fluids.

Meantime, high on Mount Kenya in the Kami Hut, Dr Oswald Oelz hoped to join the group who were going to try to get up to Gerd at dawn.

75

DR OSWALD OELZ

The others started to organise for the climb up to Gerd and prepared me plenty of hot sweet tea which was the only thing I could swallow. They were all suffering in varying degrees from mountain sickness and I didn't have high hopes for our ascent plan for the following morning.

Bert Burrage returned late in the night from the Top Hut, having done a most remarkable job in alerting the police and the Mountain Club of Kenya. He also brought down vital painkillers and penicillin.

Carrying heavy loads, Dick from Los Angeles and I started climbing very early in the morning. On the more difficult pitches we left fixed rope. By 10.00 a.m. it started to snow heavily and the climbing became increasingly difficult. I had excruciating pain in my fingers and hands which had been burned by the rope the day before. After reaching about 4900 metres Dick got very sick and exhausted from the altitude and could go no further, so we had to retreat and I lowered him with the aid of a karabiner brake, a method of running the rope through several interlinked karabiners.

I was utterly frustrated as I knew that Gerd was either dead or would be shortly and I couldn't help him. We reached the Kami Hut at night, soaked with water and snow, freezing and exhausted. Four climbers from the Mountain Club of Kenya had arrived from Nairobi during the day. They seemed to be a little sick from the rapid ascent but had brought a lot of equipment. Unfortunately there were no intravenous fluids yet, which I considered the most important medication if Gerd was still alive.

ROBERT CHAMBERS

Much of the first three days was devoted to getting plastic containers of gear up the hill. That Sunday (Day 2) was hell, an awful long slogging walk up to Kami Hut at 4400 metres (14,564 feet). We arrived to find that Oelz and an American, Richard Sykes, had tried to reach Judmaier that day and been driven back a few hundred feet from him by heavy snow. Oelz's hands were in a mess from holding Judmaier's fall and his clothes were soaked but he was very, very toughly determined to have another go.

I think it was the next morning (I am recollecting fifteen years later) that we held a crisis debate on whether to continue the rescue. Most of us were feeling dreadful, with varying degrees of mountain sickness and exhaustion, without even setting foot on the climb. In one view, to continue was irresponsible, Judmaier was probably dead already. We had learnt from Oelz how serious the fracture was. How could he survive two nights and a subsequent rescue with a badly broken leg? If we established contact with him, we would feel morally obliged to continue a rescue, although others were likely to die. Anyway we did not have the capacity to rescue him. The other view was that he might still be alive, and that a direct lower down the North Face could get him off the rocks really very fast. I was ultimately responsible for the decision.

To call off the rescue was simply not something I could bring myself to do. In fact, it did not all rest on my decision, there were some people in the party who were going to have a go anyway!

So Oelz and an MCK member, Silvano Borruso, set off on the Monday morning (Day 3) to try again to reach Judmaier. They took a radio. John Temple and Pradeep followed with the cacolet. The weather was cloudy and no pilot could see the Notch to tell whether Judmaier was still alive. I spent the day trying to acclimatise and gather strength at Kami. No message came back in the evening; there was no radio contact. And it seemed to us that Judmaier was probably dead. Morale was very low.

DR OSWALD OELZ
Silvano, the strongest climber in the group, was coming back up with me. When we reached the start of the climb we met more people who had just arrived to help. We made rapid progress, impeded only by the heavy loads.

Although Silvano was increasingly suffering from the altitude as we climbed, he followed steadily. At 5.30 p.m. more than forty-eight hours after I left Gerd, I climbed around the last ridge that separated me from his ledge, twenty metres below Shipton's Notch. I saw the shape of a motionless body covered by the red bivouac sac. Desperately I cried, 'Gerd, Gerd,' certain he would not answer. But miraculously he moved the bivouac sac from his face and said in a soft voice:

'Oh God, Bulle [my nickname] I didn't think you were still alive.' He looked desperately pale and thin. I was overwhelmed and cried into my walkie-talkie to all the people on the mountain and the whole world that he was still alive and that we could save his life if we worked fast. However the damned walkie-talkie didn't seem to work for I didn't get any response.

Gerd was suffering terrible pain and I gave him first an injection of morphine. We also gave him some fluid for his desperate thirst. He could not tolerate very much and started to vomit. In the last forty-eight hours he had had a little sip of whisky and the canned fruit which he had to open with stones, since he had lost his knife. We all three were relieved to be together, but spent a miserable cold night on the slanting rock shelf.

The morning was sunny as always and if it wasn't for the injured man we would have enjoyed that beautiful location. There were several aeroplanes flying around which told us that the rescue was well under way and that the people of Kenya cared.

After I dressed and splinted Gerd's leg, Silvano tried to carry him on his back, while John Temple, who had arrived during the morning, and I tried to assist him with two ropes. But Gerd could not tolerate the pain when the injured leg was hanging down. At least we managed to take him to a flat space which measured two metres by fifty centimetres and belay him to pitons. Gerd was looking worse than the day before, he was dying slowly. He could not take enough fluid by mouth and I still didn't have intravenous infusions.

Robert Chambers

The next morning (Day 4) Jim Hastings brought up plasma in a chopper, and landed above his normal ceiling using a saucer-shaped depression near the Kami Hut. He had stripped his machine of all but essentials. Two climbing pairs set off. Dick Cooper was in one, and I was in the other. We both carried plasma. Dick was fitter and faster. I remember that Firmin's Chimney, the crux of the climb, was long and unprotected and difficult in icy conditions.

Dr Oswald Oelz

I was sitting on the minute ledge beside Gerd, my legs hanging in space. It had started to snow again. Gerd told me that he expected to die during the night. He thought that it was terrible that it took so long to die and complained that he could not simply go to sleep for ever. During the night he developed fever and asked me to unclip him from the pitons so that he could roll over the edge and fall down the face to a quick death. (DAY 5) There was fog all around us and it was cold. There was also the noise of several planes and there was a new noise, the throb of a helicopter. Suddenly there was an almighty crash and after that there was no helicopter noise any more. We knew that it had crashed and our despair was now complete. Later we learned that the pilot, Jim Hastings, had died in the crash. Dick Cooper and another climber arrived and at last I got the essential intravenous fluids. Robert Chambers was just behind. After I set up the equipment on the rock face I injected one and a half litres. Gerd was now looking better. However, the injections started to freeze and during that night I held a Gaz stove underneath the injection bottles to enable me to give him more. From time to time I found myself thinking that it would probably be better if Gerd died now since we could not bring him down anyway. I desperately wanted to get away from this terrible place on this terrible mountain with its terrible weather.

(Day 6) The morning was very cold. There were now four climbers – John Temple, Dick Cooper, Robert Chambers and Silvano Borruso – as well as myself to help Gerd and we had enough rope to rig a cableway over the first difficult section we had to traverse. However, we failed once more to move Gerd as the pain grew unbearable when we tried. There was nothing to do but to wait for a stretcher.

ROBERT CHAMBERS

Preparations were being made for a North Face lower. From Nairobi Bob Caukwell traced 600 feet of nylon rope in Mombasa. The Kenya Police drove with it through the night over three hundred miles to Nairobi and then on to Naro Moru. It was loaded in a plane, to be dropped across the ridge. We were then to use it for the direct North Face lower. We watched the plane come, slowly excreting an extraordinarily long line, and it seemed so long it could not miss. But when released it curled and drifted and missed the ridge. So we were forced back on the wire, which would have to be dragged all the way up the long North Ridge route we had followed.

Those who had taken the stretcher to the base of the North Face reported heavy stone falls and were reluctant to bring the stretcher up by that route. The loss of the airdropped rope also meant that we would have difficulty hauling the stretcher up as we had proposed. So we decided it should come up by the Firmin-Hicks route.

Unfortunately this meant further delay, and much effort. We sent out appeals for any climbers anywhere in East Africa to come and help.

Meanwhile Dr Oelz had organised a primitive hospital ward near the summit.

DR OSWALD OELZ

I was again out of injections and painkillers and Gerd was getting rapidly worse. Covered by our bivouac sac and in the few clear moments between his fever dreams he talked about his past. He said that he had had a good life and that he was sorry to go. He complained about all the girls he had not had and all the wine he had not drunk. The snow storm in the afternoon was particularly strong and we got even more depressed. It was already dark when suddenly, like a *deus ex machina*, John Temple, who had gone down to meet the others, reappeared and told us that six Austrians were landing that night in Nairobi to help us. He also brought some plasma for intravenous injections. On my knees, partly in the open air, in darkness, with a bivouac sac that the snow storm was threatening to tear apart, I tried to insert a needle in a vein of Gerd's arm. My hands were open wounds and I couldn't feel anything but pain. I couldn't find a vein for the intravenous fluid, they were all collapsed due to the severe dehydration of my patient. After about two hours I finally succeeded in inserting the needle. I made injections throughout the night with the stove beneath the injection bottle.

ROBERT CHAMBERS

We faced a crucial decision whether to go ahead with the direct lower down down the North Face. It would have to be done

80

entirely from above, without support from below due to the stone falls which the descent would create. We debated what to do. Dick Cooper was in favour. Others were against. The party in Kami, with whom we discussed it over the radio, were strongly against. I remember sitting trying to make up my mind. The direct descent without support from below did look enormously hazardous. So we agreed on the much longer, slower and more strenuous, but safer route, along the West Ridge and then down the North Ridge, the way we had come.

Dr Oswald Oelz
Gerd had high fever and complained all the time. He asked me to make a fire and heard girls' voices, speaking German. He also told us to start to work on his evacuation immediately and not to sit around.

Robert Chambers
Different parties were now ferrying supplies up parts of the route. I worried that inexperienced climbers were going beyond their safety limits, relying on that extra verve and daring which rescues inspire. It seemed entirely possible that we would have another accident on our hands. Although Silvano Borruso was reluctant to go I sent him down. He had made a tremendous effort in the early stages of the rescue, and spent a night at 17,000 feet (over 5000 metres) with only a shirt and anorak, having given his pullover to Judmaier.

At midday on Day 7 we finally got the stretcher to Shipton's Notch and five or six of us began to try to move Judmaier. The first part was uphill. Even with the stretcher suspended from a rope in a Tirolean traverse, it took us hours to do this. The carry along the shelves of the West Ridge that followed was exhausting, and belaying was a continuous problem. But by evening, we had Judmaier at the top of the North Ridge. From here onwards, it was steeply downwards. It was a very cold and bad night for everyone, not least poor Judmaier.

Dr Oswald Oelz
It was again desperately cold and Gerd was having weird fever dreams all night. He called us drunkards and demanded some

red wine for himself too. I melted snow every two hours and tried to give it to him but he refused each time to take more than two sips.

On the Saturday (Day 8), Robert didn't think it possible for them to get Judmaier down the North Ridge.

ROBERT CHAMBERS
I had the idea of a direct lower down the Northey Glacier. We had enough rope, and the entire lower might be completed in less than an hour, providing we could organise lowering the joined ropes. I had climbed the Northey ten years earlier, and knew it had two sections of steep snow and ice separated by about fifty metres of rock fall. But the Kami party who had now done a recce were adamant that the idea was crazy. They reported very heavy stonefall, and in my slightly paranoid state by then, I wondered whether they were exaggerating in order to prevent the plan. A stronger argument was that the Austrians were coming and preferred the ridge.

DR OSWALD OELZ
That morning (Day 8) Gerd was still alive and we started to lower him down the ridge. We got down several pitches by 11.00 a.m. and then it started snowing again. I was standing with Gerd at the beginning of a sharp horizontal edge which was definitely impossible to traverse with the stretcher. While thinking about the solution to the problem I looked down the face and saw what looked like an Austrian climbing helmet approaching. I shouted down and there they were, our friends to help us. Werner Heim was first to arrive, pulling three ropes behind him. He looked so strong and trustworthy that I immediately felt that we would make it. Gerd had a moment of clarity and said, 'If you don't get me down today you're wasting your time.'

ROBERT CHAMBERS
I remember feeling that I had little left to give, and was marvelling at John Temple's resilience when there were shouts

in German, and a concentrated ball of energy burst up through the mist and snow and, within seconds, as it seemed, had rigged up ropes for lowering the stretcher. It was Werner Heim. Others came up and in no time Judmaier disappeared on his spectacular descent.

The moment the main responsibility lifted from me, I more or less collapsed for a couple of hours. I have never been so tired.

The arrival at an accident scene of a mountain rescue team from so many thousand miles away is unprecedented. All were first-class climbers with vast rescue experience on the steep cliffs of the Austrian Tirol and Dr Raimund Margreiter was a professional colleague of Gerd and Oswald. The other members of this group were Walter Larcher, Werner Heim, Kurt Pittracher, Horst Bermann and Walter Spitzenstatter.

Their assistance had been requested by Gerd's father, Professor Judmaier, who had flown out to Nairobi from Innsbruck when he got word of the accident. Upon arrival in Nairobi they first flew round Mount Kenya in a Cessna charter plane to identify Judmaier's lonely bivouac sac close to the summit of Batian.

They then landed at Nanyuki, the nearest strip to the mountain, and from there they went by Land-Rover to the Base Camp. Now with the help of porters they crossed two 4000-foot (1220-metre) passes and in forty kilometres reached the Kami Hut. It was exactly one week since the accident and they had still to climb the mountain, 600 metres of Grade IV climbing and one chimney of Grade V.

Dr Raimund Margreiter

As Walter Spitzenstatter and I got to the foot of the face we saw our friends already several rope lengths above us. Walter had had a great deal of trouble with the altitude during the ascent and we had spent a filthy cold night some two hundred metres below the Kami Hut. It was clear to us that our friends would reach Judmaier long before us and we decided, therefore, to put up a continuous abseil route as far as the Amphitheatre, in order to guarantee the evacuation even during the night. The key to this was a 200-metre rope which they had deposited at the foot of the climb. It took a long time before we had disentangled this, in order to fix it at the bottom. The other end I tied round my waist and set off.

On a rock ledge at the end of the 200 metres we fixed the rope with ten good firm pitons. After we had installed three more abseil lengths of about forty metres, we reached the Amphitheatre. The others had already brought Judmaier as far as the upper end of the Amphitheatre, where I was able to attend to his injuries. He was certainly in a very critical condition. As well as highly efficient painkillers, I administered to him the principal steroids. In order to guard against the so-called 'rescue death' which frequently hits a casualty at this point if he succumbs to the induced feeling of well-being, I tried again and again to demonstrate to him the seriousness of the situation and that he would only have to hold out a few more hours. I also gave Oswald a sip of whisky.

We continued down to the lower edge of the Amphitheatre without problem, then an abseil as far as the beginning of the 200-metre rope. Walter and I, being the last to descend, removed all the abseil points which we had only a few hours before so tiringly installed. As we came to the final abseil point at dusk it was like a nightmare: Gerd on the stretcher, surrounded by the rescuers: beneath us the endless ravine, only the first few metres of which could be seen on account of the approaching darkness. We were all aware of the risks involved on this lower and no one was keen to descend the last 200 metres with the casualty.

Werner Heim and I volunteered for this hazardous undertaking. The stretcher was attached simply to the fourteen-millimetre rope which had been untied at the bottom and pulled up; we had merely secured ourselves on to the bottom bar of the stretcher. We knew full well that on this very long descent communications were going to be difficult. Various rocket signals were agreed upon in case of emergency. And so with very mixed feelings we lowered ourselves into the darkness. To start with all went smoothly, but after twenty metres we couldn't shout up to our friends and the signalling code agreed upon didn't function either. So we had to carry the casualty to the lip of each ledge we came to. When the belayers above felt the rope go slack they eased the tension. When we then let ourselves down over the edge it meant a four- or five-metre drop each time – very unnerving. With increasing rope lengths these drops became progressively longer. Added to this, the rope dislodged stones, so that periodically a salvo would pour directly over us while we threw ourselves on top of the casualty to shield him with our bodies. The stones ricocheted off our helmets and rucksacks, which protected our backs to a degree. On one occasion the stretcher got itself stuck in a chimney, the back of which was a very steep smooth slab. As we had no footholds we could not free it despite our desperate efforts. We had a smoke and reviewed the problem, before giving it a final wrench which was rewarded with a rapid slide of a good five metres!

Fortunately for us the moon rose and improved visibility. There was however still a considerable obstacle to overcome: the eight-metre overhang at the bottom of the face. If we were to continue our abseil descent over this last pitch, we would all be hanging on the rope.

'Wait, and you'll see how safely an Austrian Army mountain guide can get you down,' Werner assured me.

After twenty frustrating minutes when periodically the rope was slackened too much, he finally succeeded in hammering a special piton in three centimetres. From this peg he then belayed me – and the casualty – down the overhang. The peg held.

In order to tell those 200 metres above of our arrival we fired a rocket. It was 10.00 p.m. Here on easier safe ground we were met by native porters and revived with tea. After a short halt Gerd was taken on to the Kami Hut accompanied by Dr Oelz. Slowly our friends emerged one after the other out of the darkness, all except Walter Spitzenstatter.

Apparently after the successful rescue he was shattered and still at the belay 200 metres above. Kurt was with him. As a rescue expert he had performed marvellously. I was horrified at the idea of having to climb up once more in the icy cold to help him through this sinister abyss. But after I had sorted out my gear I started the ascent again and eventually made contact with him by shouting. Walter was in a pitiable state and could scarcely stand. We had to support him as far as the hut, in the course of which we lost the path and unfortunately descended too far.

Robert and the other climbers were also shattered and even at this late stage there could easily have been another accident.

ROBERT CHAMBERS
For us there was now a great effort to keep concentrating and to get off the mountain safely. I had one more bivouac with two people who stayed behind. The next morning I nearly fell off on the last long abseil, which also caused others trouble.

Raimund and Kurt got back down with Walter ahead of Robert's party and Raimund was pleased to see that their effort was not in vain.

DR RAIMUND MARGREITER
In the hut Walter quickly recovered after receiving some oxygen. The rest of the night I spent caring for Judmaier: his leg appeared really bad. The still attached piece of fractured bone protruded far out of a purulent wound above the edge of the boot.

Oswald helped Raimund.

DR OSWALD OELZ
When we took Gerd's dressings off we were immediately assailed by the terrible smell of gangrene. The bone which was still protruding from the flesh was black. At first we were watched by several of the rescuers who quickly turned pale, then disappeared. Raimund and I were almost certain that Gerd would lose his leg.

DR RAIMUND MARGREITER
While I attended to his leg, Gerd celebrated his 'rebirth' with somewhat too much whisky. The excessive reaction to this

alcohol intake in his greatly enfeebled physical state was wrongly interpreted by the porters as mental derangement and a report of this was radioed to the valley. His condition next morning however permitted further evacuation.

Ruth, Oswald's girlfriend, had meanwhile arrived from Mombasa. She had first heard of the accident when she read the headline 'Is he still alive?' in a newspaper. Oswald promised her that they would spend their next holiday at a beach – 'which we never did'.

DR RAIMUND MARGREITER

Gerd was now placed on the mountain stretcher and carried in relays by four blacks. We made speedy headway. Towards midday it began to rain and the unfortunate Gerd swam, so to speak, in the bathtub of the stretcher. The wasted, bearded face with the gold-rimmed spectacles reminded me of photographs I had seen of David Livingstone: so must his natives have carried him through the bush in his time.

On Day 8 of the evacuation (13 September) Ruth and Oswald took the long drag down to the beginning of the road. 'However,' Oswald said, 'it was now very easy peaceful walking since I knew that my friend would survive and I felt the fantastic high that always comes after a big effort.'

DR RAIMUND MARGREITER

Aeroplanes repeatedly circled over us dropping messages: 'Hang on, only another five miles, the whole of Kenya is praying for you.'

We were moved by this, the sympathy of a whole country. In the late afternoon we reached the main camp, where Gerd met his father who had organised the whole operation so magnificently. The further journey by jeep to the airstrip at Nanyuki, the flight to Nairobi, and the medical operation had all been well prepared and thought out beforehand.

A farmer took Oswald and Ruth in his four-wheel-drive car through the mud to his farm in the plains. Here, for the first time in ten days,

*the doctor relaxed. Next morning they got the good news that Gerd
had been operated on in Nairobi and that he still had his leg!*

*Robert Chambers considers the rescue in retrospect. It is the summing
up of a modest man.*

ROBERT CHAMBERS
We would have been faster if we had decided on the North
Ridge from the start: but then it would have been harder to
believe we could ever get Gerd off the mountain that way and
we might have given up. We would have been faster if we had
never relied on the cacolet stretcher; but we did not know till
we tried. Gerd would have been off quicker if we had called
out the Austrians at the start; but it never occurred to us then
that a team could come all the way from Europe. Jim Hastings
the helicopter pilot would not have died if there had been no
rescue bid, but in the event he did not die in vain, and there was
no way there could have been no rescue. That was fate. The
balance sheet in lives, at the end, was one for one, and it could
easily have been worse. But to count lives seems wrong. Some
things just have to be done. What I see now, and did not at the
time, is how much we owed to the Austrians. If they had not
come, I believe Judmaier would have died on the mountain,
quite likely with some of us. His father expressed gratitude to
us, but we should also thank him; for he and the Austrian
climbers released us from the rescue, and perhaps in turn saved
some of us.

The last words are with Oswald:
Ten years later we celebrated Gerd's 'tenth anniversary' with a
superb climb in the Tirol. The previous evening we enjoyed
both the wine and the company of our girlfriends. It was an
anniversary to remember.

5

HIGH WINDS IN THE ANDES

Acclimatisation is possibly the greatest single factor involved in accidents on the world's highest mountains. If the members of the casualty's climbing party can be deployed, well and good, but if the rescue party has to come from much lower, the rescuers themselves are put at considerable risk from pulmonary or cerebral oedema, in addition to the danger of moving on difficult ground when suffering from mountain sickness.

This rescue story is from Chile, along the border with Argentina, on a mountain called Ojos del Salado, at 6885 metres (22,590 feet) the second-highest peak in the Americas and the highest active volcano in the world.

I first heard about this accident from Bob Lyall, an expatriot Scot now living in Santiago. Bob is one of the prospecting bosses of the Anglo-American Corporation and has an avid interest in mountaineering. He called in at my home in Glencoe when on holiday in Scotland in 1985, and was telling me enthusiastically about a great volcanic complex he discovered when poring over NASA photographs taken from space. The company use these photographs for studying terrain with possible mineral deposits. The year before they had used them for a grimmer purpose. Bob told me the story.

It was in April 1984 when Louis George Murray visited Chile to see the Anglo-American projects at first hand. Louis was a geologist and a senior executive in the company, based in South Africa. He had a passion for the wide open spaces of the world and a talent for photographing them.

Both Louis and Bob Lyall were suffering from bad backs at the time, legacies of countless miles in four-wheel-drive vehicles over rough and roadless terrain. With this in mind, Bob arranged for a helicopter to take Louis round the various projects in the mountains to the east of Copiapó, which is some eight hundred kilometres north of the capital, Santiago.

As Ojos del Salado was such a fascinating geological phenomenon, Bob suggested that it should be included in the itinerary as it could be overflown after a visit to Esperanza, which is the most northerly of the company's prospecting camps. The helicopter chosen for this flying visit was a Lama belonging to Helicopters Andes, a company whose pilots have vast experience of high-altitude work. César Tejos, an ex-Commander of the Chilean Air Force in Antarctica, was to be their 'driver'.

When César was asked if it would be possible to overfly Ojos summit with the helicopter, he consulted his tables and told Bob and Louis that it would be feasible with two passengers and a minimum supply of fuel, although a landing was out of the question. Even if a landing had been on, it would be unwise to leave the aircraft as anyone could collapse within a few seconds if suddenly deprived of the Lama's oxygen supply at that height.

Bob Lyall and Louis Murray started their inspection of the prospecting camps on 14 April and the following morning a pick-up truck was sent with Tomás Vila to Laguna Verde, a lake close to the mountain, with fuel for the Ojos flights. That same day the helicopter left Esperanza camp with Robert Schnell, Enrique Viteri, Louis and Bob on board. The mechanic was left at the camp to monitor the helicopter radio frequency.

Just after 8.00 a.m. they located the pick-up at Laguna Verde and, after refuelling, Bob and Roberto set off on the first recce flight. Conditions were perfect and the Lama climbed high over the arid terrain, which is really the southern end of the Atacama Desert, and without trouble circled the summit twice and angled back down to the emerald-green lake. Though the weather was superb with clear, windless skies, it was confirmed that a landing on the summit was out of the question as the temperature was −15°C, comparatively mild for the end of the South American summer.

In order to keep the helicopter as light as possible, it had been decided that Louis would do the second flight alone with César, and they took off at 10.20 a.m. The others at the edge of the lake watched the helicopter diminish in size until it was a mere speck in the azure sky.

When the Lama hadn't returned by 11.30 a.m. they became worried, especially as they had no radio contact with the helicopter from the pick-up. At midday Tomás and Enrique drove west a few miles to get a better view of Ojos, but by 2.00 p.m. they returned having seen no sign of the Lama.

Bob Lyall had thought there was an outside chance that some minor mechanical fault had developed and César had considered it safer to return to the camp and his mechanic, rather than go back to Laguna Verde. So there was only one course left, to go to Esperanza, about 120 kilometres, to see if the helicopter had returned there. Once more Tomás and Enrique climbed into the pick-up and set off, while Bob and Roberto took up temporary residence in the old abandoned Chile–Argentina frontier post, constructed in natural caves by Laguna Verde.

At 4 p.m. the pick-up arrived at Esperanza and after speaking with the mechanic, who had had no radio contact with the Lama either, they realised that the helicopter was indeed missing. Santiago was then contacted and Helicopters Andes confirmed a First Stage alert with the National Search and Rescue Organisation of the Chilean Air Force. Some of the fittest personnel from the camp were mustered and arrived at the carabineiro post about 7 p.m. Following in their tracks on the long dusty road, which climbs to over 15,000 feet, were other essential supplies and equipment: radios, food, bedding, generator, flares. Word arrived that a Cheyenne aircraft as well as the helicopter company's second Lama (Kilo Alpha) would depart Santiago 6.00 a.m. next day to assist them. About to commence was the highest search operation ever conducted in the Americas.

On any rescue operation, especially in big mountains, there can be confusion and false leads to follow and eliminate, wasting valuable time. Such was the case for the ground party, led by Enrique Viteri, which set off to reach a mountaineers' refuge at 16,700 feet (5100 metres), on the lower slopes of Ojos del Salado. This was a logical move, for one can't always rely on air search, especially at high altitude, and it was assumed that had the helicopter made a forced landing and the two men survived, they would have headed towards this known place of shelter. For to spend a night in the open without special clothing at such a height would be courting disaster. On the first flight with Bob and Roberto, César had pinpointed the yellow-painted refuge.

However, Enrique's party had trouble finding the hut in the dark. Previous parties had driven up there with four-wheel-drive vehicles, choosing whatever route took their fancy over the dunes, with the result that the place resembled a twin-tracked maze. It was not until they had radioed Eduardo Olmedo, a mountaineer who knew the area well, that they managed to locate the refuge at about 9 p.m. On the way one of the party reported a white flare to the south-east.

Various flares were set off in reply, but there was no response to these. There was further confusion when the flares which they had fired were in turn reported as from the missing helicopter.

The white-flare sighting (it was established later that this must have been a shooting star) spurred the Ojos rescue team into setting off up the mountain from the hut at 10 p.m. It was full moon and below them the vast expanse of open country was broken only by the white heads of the mountains. Laguna Verde lay in the shadow of a hollow between hills. They reached a height of 20,300 feet (6200 metres) by dawn and searched into the next day, Sunday, without success.

As promised the Cheyenne fixed-wing plane arrived in the area at 8.00 a.m., but base at Laguna Verde had no direct communication with it. From the mountainside Enrique could make indirect contact by first radioing the Andes Lama helicopter, which was now airborne and heading up the narrow torso of Chile to Copiapó en route for the mountain. This way he could relay messages from base at Laguna Verde, where Bob Lyall and other members of Anglo-American were still ensconced in the subterranean guard post. The Cheyenne pilot was Pablo Pfingsthron, a man with 29,000 flying hours behind him and the co-pilot Jorge Lathrop, Director of Helicopters Andes.

Bob asked them to check out craters and fumaroles in the summit area, just in case they had landed safely and Louis's fascination with geology and photography had lured him to these features. The Cheyenne searched the summit area until its fuel was getting low then returned to La Serena to fill up. In the afternoon it again quartered Ojos, but still they didn't see any sign of the missing Lama, although false hopes were raised when they spotted red-jacketed figures on the mountain, to be dispelled when walkie-talkie and radio contacts established that they were, in fact, Enrique's team.

The Chilean Search and Rescue organisation were meanwhile deploying a Twin Otter and another Lama from the base at Antofagasta. Commander Heinrich was in charge of the official SAR and he asked José Miguel Infante, Helicopters Andes Operations Manager, to co-ordinate with him. But as José arrived in Copiapó in the company Lama ahead of the SAR group he refuelled and carried on to Laguna Verde where he touched down at 4 p.m. and managed one search mission before dark, covering the ground between the summit and Laguna Verde.

That Sunday night the rescuers got into their sleeping bags somewhat despondent and there was another false report of a flare, this time on the north side of Laguna Verde. The old frontier post was busier than it had been for years and the twin caverns echoed with the plans of the rescuers. Mixed teams of company men, carabineiro and police were selected to search on both sides of the border, but the Argentinian authorities would give permission only for civilian teams, so the next day an Anglo-American Company contingent under Tomás Vila was to cross the border to search the south-eastern flank of the peak. The police and army were ordered to Laguna Negro Francisco on the other side of Ojos to commence search operations there.

Up in the refuge the hope which the Anglo-American party had felt the previous night had now, after an exhausting day's search, been replaced with a numbness. They realised that Louis and César would have to be very lucky to be still alive. Their own situation was one of acute frustration. Though they were used to working at 14,000 feet or so, the extra altitude was telling. Acclimatisation is essential and in normal circumstances should be attained by slow degrees, not by a relentless push to over 20,000 feet. Every step had been an effort, yet colleagues in distress are a compelling incentive.

However they could do no more good on the mountain and returned to base.

The next day, a Monday, was a day which the aircrews of the Ojos del Salado rescue won't forget. It was a day of high wind and turbulence.

José was airborne first in the Lama, with Enrique as observer, and checked out the wild country to the north and north-west of Laguna Verde. It was in this region that the flare had been reported the previous evening, but they found nothing. By 8.00 a.m. the SAR Twin Otter started on its search pattern, while José in the Lama was on his second patrol of the day. Both aircraft were still operating within Chilean territory, but by 11.00 a.m. permission came through to overfly Argentina and José immediately swung over the divide to concentrate his efforts on the south side of the mountain. Flying conditions were appalling – the prevailing westerly winds, warmed by their passage over the Atacama desert, stream over the chain of high peaks which form the border, to descend in the notorious 'mountain wave' on the Argentinian side. The turbulence behind the mountains was terrific, and José had to use all his skills to keep the Lama flying. At one point they were hurtled downwards at 4000 feet per minute, and José wrestled the machine south towards the broad flat expanse of the Salina de la Laguna Verde, contemplating a forced landing, while Enrique radioed their position to Bob at base. However, conditions improved a little, and, all possibility of a systematic search having gone, José concentrated his efforts on solving their own predicament, and gradually worked his way back until he managed to slip over a pass some fifty kilometres west of Ojos del Salado, into the welcoming rising air on the Chilean side of the mountains, to angle back to base at Laguna Verde, exhausted by the tensions of what he later described as the worst experience of his flying career.

The press can be a mixed blessing on any protracted rescue. Often they get in the way, jam switchboards vital for communications and get the facts wrong. In all fairness, however, they often do good by publicising the plight of rescue teams in dire need of donations. On the Ojos del Salado rescue, however, the common radio frequency chosen by the

SAR authorities for the emergency was Anglo-American's 7790. Once this was known, the frequency was monitored by radio hams and also by a broadcasting station. So Bob's contact back to the mining camps as well as SAR information was monitored and sent out for public consumption.

A report was made to the local Intendente in Copiapó that a helicopter had landed at approximately 11.00 a.m. on the 14th close by Cerro El Gato, about 150 kilometres south-west of Ojos. Those at base were somewhat sceptical about this sighting, for it was doubtful if the missing Lama had sufficient fuel to get that far. Also the same helicopter had been working in that particular area a week previously. The sighting could have been confused. Nevertheless, after José's narrow escape that day such a possibility couldn't be discounted, for there was a stock of helicopter fuel at Aldebarán camp and José had spotted a pass which led there via Laguna Negro Francisco, which could provide a bolt hole for an aircraft in trouble. The Argentinians were now in action using a Hercules as a spotter plane crammed with observers. They had also a couple of Lamas standing by should they have any positive results. Help was now coming from all quarters and patrols were out to the north and west on the mountain, as well as Tomás Vila's group on the Argentinian side.

More oxygen for use in the Lama and climbing equipment arrived that evening, which meant that the Anglo-American party which was going back up Ojos now had better gear to tackle the upper regions of the mountain, and this time instead of using the Ojos refuge as an advanced base they pushed up higher and set up camp at 20,300 feet (6200 metres).

On the Wednesday Bob Lyall returned to Santiago, leaving Enrique in charge on the spot, and he asked his second in command, Iain Thomson, to arrange photographic coverage of the mountain. Bob felt that studying enlargements might give them the best chance of locating the missing helicopter. This is a sound idea provided one can ensure comprehensive coverage from enough angles. For it is notoriously difficult and tiring to concentrate on searching what is often a hypnotic landscape in turbulent conditions from the air.

The photographic flight was set in motion but ran into such turbulence that most of the photographers spent the time being violently sick, and took two days to complete their assignment.

Meanwhile the Anglo-American party which had camped high on Ojos was not faring so well. One of the team was a small agile geophysicist and surveyor called Carlos Pérez and I was later to observe his ability as a natural mountaineer. Carlos' nickname in the mining camps is Darling, a word which he frequently uses to supplement his limited English vocabulary. With five colleagues Carlos had set off from their tents at 20,300 feet in an attempt to gain the summit. Now at 10.30 a.m. and a height of 21,000 feet, only one other member of the party was fit to go on. The others had succumbed to altitude sickness. Above, after negotiating a difficult section on rock and ice, his remaining companion fell victim to sickness and exhaustion and Carlos told him to return to camp.

At 5 p.m. Carlos reached a cairn between the two summits and saw, close by a section of disturbed snow, a small weighted company pennant which Louis had prepared to jettison on the summit as they flew over. The objective of his climb was to search the summit and also to look down the east side, but due to a ferocious wind and driving snow he couldn't get to the eastern summit. He put the flag in his pocket, and decided to return to their high camp, but didn't reach this until 11 p.m., so exhausted that he had to be carried the last few hundred metres to camp by his companions, who had heard him call for help. The temperature on the summit that day was −20°C.

Next morning, Friday, the photographic crew were airborne once more and completed their mission. By the evening all the material was processed and being studied in Santiago by Bob. There seemed to be two areas worth closer investigation. One photograph showed what looked like human figures close to an area of hot springs and the other showed skid marks on the snow.

Added to this, the news that Carlos had found the flag on the summit confirmed that the Lama had in fact reached the top of Ojos, probably a little over half an hour after take-off. This meant that, calculating from the Lama's depleted fuel reserves, the search could now be concentrated in a much tighter area round the mountain.

The West Face of Siula Grande. **O** = snow caves; XI = where Joe Simpson was injured on descent of North Ridge; X2 = point where Simon Yates was forced to cut the rope holding Joe Simpson.

A painful descent by mule with the right leg splinted in a Karrimat.

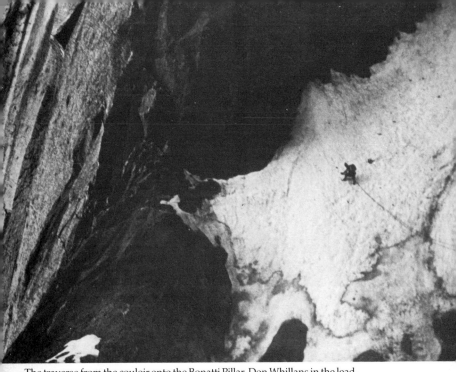

The traverse from the couloir onto the Bonatti Pillar, Don Whillans in the lead.

The Aiguille Verte and the Drus. BP = the
Bonatti Pillar; W = the West Face; C = the start
of the couloir.

Members of the Chamonix rescue team on the
Petit Dru.

Mount Kenya from the north: **x** marks Judmaier's accident position; dotted line shows direct descent route considered and rejected as too prone to stonefall; ▲ bivouac at end of Day 7; **A** marks where the Austrians joined the rescue on Day 8.

A close-up of the rescue area below Shipton's Notch. **T** marks the rope for the Tyrolean Traverse, and **x** shows one of the rescuers. Judmaier's ledge is just to left of leftmost **T**.

Gerd Judmaier about to be flown to hospital in Nairobi.

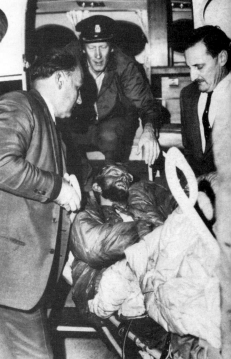

Four rescued climbers roped up and being led to the pick-up point on Beinn an Dothaidh.

A Sea King helicopter arrives to evacuate them in very bad January conditions.

Henderson's body was found on Beinn Achaladair at the point marked **x** which corresponds with the 'spirit' map **x** at 3000 feet. Achallader farm is at the foot of the mountain, right.

Duncan Smith of Achallader farm who found the body.

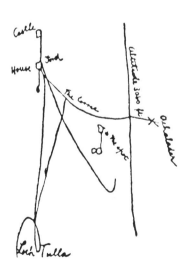

Mount Washington showing the main gullies O-Odell's; P-Pinnacle; C-Central; D-Diagonal.

Hugh Herr, adjusting a climbing foot.

A hard dangerous lead on his artificial feet in 19

The White Elbe valley in the Giant Mountains, from Meadow Chalet.

The North Face of Mieguszowiecki, High Tatra.

High Peak 12,349 ft   Middle Peak 12,210 ft   Porter Col   Low Peak 11,787 ft

Upper Empress Shelf 10,000 ft

9000 ft

Lower Empress Shelf

Mount Cook from the west. ✘ marks Middle Peak Hotel, occupied from 16-29 November 1982 by Phil Doole and Mark Inglis; ▲ marks Empress advance base and site of helicopter crash.

Don Bogie bringing in Phil Doole to Upper Empress Shelf on a strop under the Squirrel helicopter.

Phil Doole (right) with Mark Inglis on the stretcher being checked by a rescuer at the snow cave on the Upper Empress Shelf.

Iain Thomson made another flight as observer in the Cheyenne on Saturday the 21st and checked the two suspicious areas spotted in the photographs. Both proved negative.

That day, about lunchtime, Louis Murray's son, Michael, arrived in Santiago from South Africa and spent the remainder of the day and that night with Bob Lyall and family. It was arranged to fly him over the Ojos area the following morning to show him where his father and César went missing. At dawn the Cheyenne took off with Henry Stucke, Anglo's technical director for Latin America, who had come over from Sao Paulo, Iain Thomson and Michael on board. When they were overflying the eastern side of the summit the pilot Pablo Pfingsthron glimpsed a brief flash of light, on a patch of snow high on the mountain. They circled and Iain Thomson was able to recognise the missing Lama. There was no sign of life. SAR in Copiapó and the ground parties were advised of the find. The Twin Otter and the helicopters were scrambled and homed in on the location which was at 22,000 feet. As the Twin Otter tried to approach, closer than the Cheyenne was able, the wind was registering 100 knots and the plane was actually moving backwards at one stage. The helicopters couldn't get to the crashed Lama either, but they managed to report that the machine seemed more or less intact and there didn't appear to be anyone inside. This raised the hopes of the rescuers once more, for they knew that if Louis and César had managed to use the oxygen on board the helicopter, and get to the heat-giving fumaroles, they might just have survived the otherwise low temperatures. For the rest of the day flying conditions were desperate. Once Henry had described the location of the crash, 'a snow patch like a map of South America, with the Lama in the position of Buenos Aires', Bob easily spotted the aircraft in several photographs, which goes to show that specialised knowledge is just as essential for interpreting aerial photographs as for on-the-spot search.

Flying conditions were better on Monday the 23rd, and the Twin Otter was able to make a near pass to the crashed helicopter and later a Lama flew close in. A figure wearing an orange jacket was still in the passenger's seat, but the exact position of Louis was difficult to establish.

Now all energy was concentrated on getting climbing

parties to the crash and after a great deal of effort, between 27 April and 2 May, members of the Santiago rescue group, Cuerpo de Socorro Andino, under Alejo Contreras Stateding, together with Anglo-American personnel, succeeded in reaching the Lama. They had been instructed by SAR only to photograph the situation. In fact, the machine was so delicately balanced that there was a danger of it falling over if they had tried to recover the bodies. Both men must have died instantly in the impact, which had also sheared off the automatic electronic distress beacon.

There remained the formidable task of recovering the bodies of the victims, for early May is the start of winter in the area, with lowering summit temperatures, higher winds, and the possibility of severe snow storms. However, the Anglo-American team were determined to complete the task, if at all possible – they were fit and acclimatised, but lacked the technical experience necessary. So they engaged the support of four experienced Chilean mountaineers, led by Jorge Quinteros, and now, well equipped and organised, set out once again towards the summit. A bulldozer was called in, which cut a track suitable for four-wheel-drive vehicles from the refuge at the base of the mountain to a height of about 20,000 feet, and the bulldozer itself managed to assist in transporting equipment to Carlos' camp site at 20,300 feet. By 12 May, the helicopter had toppled over in the wind and in two separate expeditions, the bodies were recovered and taken down for burial.

As a tribute to Louis Murray, Anglo-American built the Louis Murray Lodge at 15,000 feet close to Laguna Verde on the wide-open desert country, and installed a new climbers' refuge, dedicated to César Tejos, at the end of the road up the mountain built during the rescue operation. It has never been established with certainty what caused the crash, but recently parts of the engine have been salvaged, possibly the highest salvage operation ever.

6

SIXTY YEARS ON BEINN ACHALADAIR

These stories of Beinn Achaladair span a period of sixty years, and they are linked by some curious coincidences of people and places.

The mountain seems insignificant enough, a well-rounded heap of grass, scree and rock in summer. In winter it is popular with hillwalkers, but not something to take a rope to, though its seemingly innocuous slopes are often subject to icing.

Beinn Achaladair is one of several mountains which stand to the east of Loch Tulla, the large natural water receptacle on the southern fringe of the Moor of Rannoch. The West Highland railway line skirts the bottom of the face, giving it the appearance from across the valley of some great force trying to undercut the mountain. Further up this line a group of bowler-hatted railway engineers once nearly succumbed to a blizzard when prospecting the rail route to Fort William. It goes without saying that the area should not be treated casually by walkers, bowler-hatted or otherwise; winter storms can be sudden and severe.

For the purpose of relating these case histories, we start in 1983 and go back in time.

Icy Rocks and Windswept Boulders

On 12 November of that year I went to an exhibition of paintings by the artist William Cadenhead in Edinburgh. In the gallery I was approached by a tall man who announced himself as one of four climbers the Glencoe Rescue Team had

99

rescued a few years previously from Beinn an Dothaidh, one of Beinn Achaladair's close neighbours. I remembered the incident well and was glad to see that he, for one, seemed none the worse for his encounter with the mountain or our team.

The reason for my journey to Edinburgh on that cold 12 November was twofold. In addition to artistic exposure, I was also there to visit and photograph that august Victorian structure, the Royal Bank of Scotland in Exchange Square. This strange assignment stemmed from three Amazonian expeditions in search of Inca gold, tenuous clues about which had led me from the arrow grass of the Llanganatis of Ecuador to this edifice of prosperity. Certain documents suggested that part of the Incan hoard had found its way by a devious route to the coffers of this most Royal Bank.

Having taken my photograph, visited the art gallery and bidden farewell to Bill Cadenhead and the rescuee, I drove back to Glencoe, passing a bleak cloud-covered Beinn Achaladair en route, and as I sped along the A82, between Loch Tulla and Beinn Achaladair, my thoughts took me back over the rescues on the mountain.

I had just arrived home when Willie Elliot opened the door. As the Glencoe Ranger, Willie looks after the property of the National Trust for Scotland, an area embracing most of the glen. He and his brother Walter have been rescuing people off the local mountains since they were boys, though they are not climbers in the rope and ice-axe mould.

'Aye, Hamish. There's a call-out near Beinn Achaladair. I got a call from Jimmy Bannerman. He was contacted by the Oban Police.'

Jimmy Bannerman was our local policeman.

'Well, I suppose it's back across the Rannoch Moor, Willie. What's the score?'

'I've got a map reference, it seems as if a chap's fallen to the north of Achaladair on Meall Buidhe, but I don't have any more gen.'

'OK, Willie, call out the boys and we'll meet at Achallader farm. Can you arrange for both the truck and the Land-Rover to be taken over?'

Up until 1975, Beinn Achaladair was within the Glencoe Mountain Rescue Team's jurisdiction under the Argyll County

Police, but after regionalisation, it came under the umbrella of Strathclyde, a large area administered from Glasgow. As assistance from Glencoe hadn't been requested immediately, by the time we got to Achallader farm, the Strathclyde Police Mountain Rescue Team had arrived from the Divisional Headquarters in Dumbarton, over sixty miles distant, together with police from Oban.

It was dark by now and visibility was very poor due to cloud cover above 2000 feet. We set off, armed with the map reference. There were about ten Glencoe Team members and Willie set up base in our truck close to the farm buildings. Achallader farm had been run by the Smith family for two generations. Both father and son were involved in these stories.

A problem that dull typical November Saturday was that the telephones in the area were out of order. Consequently the survivor of the accident, a Dr Manson, had to drive sixteen miles to Crianlarich to raise the alarm. Apparently he and his companion, John Burke, were hillwalking when, close to the summit of Meall Buidhe, Burke's bootlace came undone. Dr Manson strolled slowly on, assuming his friend would catch him up. On looking back, however, the doctor saw to his horror that his companion had strayed to the edge of the north-west face and fallen over. Dr Manson tried to see where his colleague had landed but the ground was steep and festooned with rock faces. He descended, cutting round the bottom of the face with difficulty. Finding no sign of his friend, he decided the best course of action was to get help. He immediately set off for Achallader farm, where he discovered that the telephones were out of order.

This, together with the map reference, was all the information we could muster.

We did a sweep search up the open corrie leading to the map reference; the police on the left flank, the north side, and the Glencoe Team on the valley floor and to the right, the south side. The group I was with eventually joined a police party as the valley narrowed and we stopped all together for a breather. Discussing the problem with some of them, I mentioned that the name of the man who fell was John Burke, that he worked in banking and was a regular visitor to Glencoe.

'John Burke? John Burke?' A policeman was searching his memory for something. 'Surely the signature John Burke is on the Royal Bank of Scotland notes?'

Those who had wallets quickly took these out and looked through our paper money. Sure enough several of us had notes with Burke's signature on them.

As we moved into the head of the corrie, visibility became worse and our headlamp beams diffused in the dense cloud. After several hours' search there was still no sign of the missing man and we had a further discussion. The police team decided to call it a day, return to base and recommence the search at first light. They planned to stay at Bridge of Orchy Hotel for the night. I told them we would pack it in after we had completed a quick once-over at the bottom of the topmost cliffs. Most of our team are climbers so this was easier for us to do as the ground was steep and treacherous. A short time later, Peter Weir reported over his radio that he had just come across a formidable landslide, no doubt a result of torrential rains which had washed the Highlands over the previous weeks.

I and a few others followed a weakness in the cliffs to the west of this, which leads up steeply in a grassy ramp interspersed with rocky outcrops. But here the cloud was so thick we could barely see ten feet. Meanwhile, the rest of the team in the corrie below were getting the itchy feet associated with a lost cause, so I too decided to call things off for the night. Searching in such conditions was really farcical.

The call-out for the next day was at first light, which during November in Scotland doesn't mean an early start. Alan Thomson, Richard Grieve and I were the first to arrive at Achallader. In the gloom we could see the lights of an RAF Wessex helicopter landing at the farm. It had flown from Glenmore Lodge in the Cairngorms where there was a weekend rescue exercise.

The winchman came over as I pulled up. He had to shout above the helicopter's still-running engines. 'We've found the man. He's dead and in a difficult place. Can a couple of you come up and give us a hand?'

We found John Burke at the bottom of the face we had been on a few hours previously. He had plunged across the ramp we had climbed and smashed into the top of the landslide.

Difficult enough to spot in daylight, he would have been almost impossible to see at night as he lay at the bottom of the rock face in a field of boulders. Apparently the helicopter flew directly to the map reference en route to Achallader farm and had spotted the dead man immediately. A fine bit of mountain rescue search work.

Once Alan and I were winched down on steep scree below where Burke lay, we quickly climbed up and brought him to a point where the pilot managed to lower the winch wire. The rotors were literally a few feet from the cliff, but thank goodness it was a still day. Otherwise, as the pilot said later, he wouldn't have been in there at all.

That was the end of that particular incident, and unfortunately, the end of a remarkable man. John Burke was highly respected in financial circles throughout the country. The mountains and the freedom of the hills were to him a release from the pressures of big business. In solitude he could lose the responsibilities of his office. In so doing, he lost his life.

After his body was taken away in the ambulance, John Grieve, Richard's brother, recalled another local story about John Burke. A couple of years back he had been staying at the Onich Hotel while on a climbing holiday in the Glencoe region. At the end of his stay he asked the receptionist for his bill, and wrote a cheque for the amount. When she asked for his bank card, he had to confess that he had left it at home. She insisted that she couldn't accept a cheque without the card. John Burke then took a ten-pound note from his wallet and, handing it to the girl, asked if she would kindly compare his signature on the cheque with that on the note.

It never ceases to surprise me how coincidence, as well as fate, seems so much part and parcel of rescue work. Earlier that year, above Crianlarich, where Dr Manson went to raise the alarm for his fallen friend, two climbers had fallen and been killed. One of these, Alan Jessiman, was the Chairman of the Bank of Scotland, another eminent Scottish bank.

Now we must go back to an unlucky 13 January in 1977. Four climbers from the Grampian Club of Dundee set off to climb a gully on Beinn an Dothaidh, a close neighbour of Ben Achaladair. The northerly aspect of this peak is known locally to Gaelic-speakers as the 'clenched fist' from its tight formation of gullies and buttresses.

When they failed to return I got a call from the Oban Police. It was bleak weather with soft snow above 1500 feet and an icy south-easterly wind. There is little daylight in these high latitudes during January, and dusk had fallen when we left Achallader farm. It was the sort of evening we would have preferred to be sitting by our respective fires.

The RAF Leuchars Mountain Rescue team had already searched in vain. Now it was our turn. We split into three groups, each taking a different area, but all three parties initially heading up the Allt Coire Achaladair to gain our respective search blocks to the south of Beinn Achaladair.

Ian McCrae, a local gamekeeper who knows every nook and cranny in these mountains, was with us. We spread out with our headlamps on as we ascended from the valley floor forming a wide sweeping, overlapping line of light. Further up, it was even colder and windier. The blast cultivated spindrift, making it appear as if we were walking on a shallow white foaming sea. After four hours we had to call it a night and return to search at first light.

At Achallader farm the following morning we found that the police had mustered reinforcements, with teams drawn from various parts of the Strathclyde Region as well as rescue dogs. The RAF Leuchars team were also back.

A helicopter which had been promised for first light got diverted en route for a serious accident in the hills above Crianlarich, but it was hoped that it would come later in the day. Some of the police top brass had arrived and I suggested they request a Naval Sea King helicopter. These are based at Prestwick where they are normally used for anti-submarine patrol work in the North Atlantic.

'We'll be needing white sticks in that crap above, how's a bloody chopper going to fly?' commented one of the lads as we struggled back up towards the cliffs of Beinn an Dothaidh.

But fly it did, in horizontal driving snow and nil visibility.

We spread out in line to sweep up the corrie, really a sloping shoulder with a depression in it, treading up left towards the summit. Ian Nicholson and Ed Grindley went off to the left to check the principal gully climb on the face and the plan was, by the time they had done this, we would hopefully have swung round to meet them on the summit. But they found the climbing too dangerous, due to the high avalanche risk.

Our hunch of this corrie the previous evening paid off. We heard a call, which sounded unreal – but it was a call for help. It came from the gully and through a window in the cloud we saw a figure emerge from the snow at the last pitch. Then another, then a third.

It was obvious that our best course of action was to tackle the problem from above, and after making radio contact with base, Ian McCrae as the fastest man on the hill this side of Tyndrum, volunteered to bring up the 500-foot rescue rope.

By the time we got things organised on the top and had ascertained (by shouting) that the trapped climbers below were uninjured, Ian McCrae was spotted with the long rope toiling through snow-choked boulders.

We had learned by now from the climbers that the leader had fallen 150 feet, but fortunately the rope snagged. This possibly saved them all from plunging to the valley below. The leader, though uninjured, didn't relish the thought of retackling the final pitch of the gully, which was at a high angle, and capped with a formidable cornice. As descent was also dangerous, he had wisely chosen to stay with his less experienced companions. They found a suitable bivouac spot behind a snowed-up chockstone infinitely more snug than our windswept nocturnal venue.

When the rope arrived I grabbed an end and, inching over to the cornice, cut a V in the snow. I then chucked some coils down, shouting to those below for one of them to tie on. After about five long cold minutes we heard a faint cry which we interpreted as 'OK'. The team didn't need any prompting; all were wanting to get to hell out of this wind-blasted place as it was bitterly cold. They started to pull in line, each grasping the non-stretch Terylene rope in ice-coated mitts like a snowman tug of war team.

I stayed close to the edge, monitoring the lift, and gave my radio to one of the younger team members to relay the operation to base. He hadn't used a radio in such a public way before and was obviously nervous with so many 'high hed yins' at base.

The haul rope bit into the snow edge as effectively as a cheese cutter. My shouts of 'Hold it! Hold it, for God's sake!' were snatched by the wind. Also the lads were finding it more expedient to run backwards with the rope, rather than pull it in from a static position; their crampons afforded excellent traction. After a few seconds I could barely see the closest snowman hauler through the swirling snow.

But where I had failed by command, compression and friction on the rope in the root of the cornice succeeded in slowing up the rising man. Now the rope strained to a halt. I could see melt water from the ice exuding from it. It was obviously in considerable tension.

Suddenly, just in front of my crampons, the snow surface exploded and a balaclava'd head shot out of the hole as if fired from a cannon on the floor of the corrie. The first man had been rescued!

He was none the worse for his adventure, and like a patient who'd had an aching tooth extracted, seemed glad it was all over.

The subsequent hauls, though perhaps not so dramatic, were certainly faster as there was no cornice left to hamper the team's efforts. The last man, who was also the lightest, materialised on the plateau at speed, appropriately wearing snow goggles.

While this was going on I had forgotten all about the young team member who was relaying our progress to base. It wasn't until years later that I discovered that his commentary had caused great consternation in the upper echelons of the Strathclyde Police Department. Every few minutes or so, they had received a sombre message.

'First fatality now up.'

'Second fatality now up.' And so on, until four had been effectively dealt with. Only then did he realise his mistake, hurriedly adding, 'I mean climber, not fatality.'

Right on cue, we heard from base that a Sea King was approaching, and asking if it could be of assistance.

'Yes please,' I replied. 'The climbers we pulled up may be suffering from hypothermia. We'll take them to the west of the summit to see if visibility's better. I'll call you in fifteen minutes, over.'

Some of the RAF Leuchars team had joined us by now and they could contact the chopper on their frequency.

We helped the four stiff men across the plateau, hoping for a window which would allow the Sea King to approach.

At the westerly side it was clearer, and we could see down the slope for about fifty yards or so, through a very small opening in the cloud. Below, the edge of Loch Tulla materialised. We could also discern the large brown and black camouflaged helicopter, outlined above the water. I hurriedly took a bearing on it and asked one of the RAF lads to relay the back bearing of this to the pilot so that he could approach. Just as this was done, the cloud socked in again, but we could hear the machine approach, though too far to our left. It wasn't until later I realised that when I snatched the bearing I had been standing alongside Alan Thomson, a keen photographer, and his exposure meter must have affected the compass. Fortunately the Sea King is equipped with radar and it nosed its way along the ridge. Then the cloud cleared sufficiently for the pilot to spot us. It was a bold piece of flying.

At that time we didn't have much experience with large helicopters and the downwash took us by surprise, blowing several of us over. Luckily, the plateau was wide and there was no danger. The four frigid climbers were bundled aboard and, as there was plenty of room, several of us joined them. In minutes we were back at base.

It was a good rescue, no one was hurt, and I for one wouldn't have missed the sight of the first climber's head breaking through that cornice for anything.

Next we go back just over a decade to a crisp January night in 1966. In those days we couldn't rely on much being done for us by the paraffin budgie, as helicopters were known to the rescue teams. It made for a tremendous team spirit however when everything on a call-out was down to us.

I had just finished dinner after seven hard hours on the hill, and decided to pick up an Agatha Christie novel, *The Labours of Hercules*. The title seemed most appropriate, for that day I had hauled four climbing-course members up a new route in Glencoe's Lost Valley.

In Glencoe, we get two distinct types of conditions for

accidents. The first is heavy snow cover with bad weather conditions, when people either get caught in storms or are avalanched, or both. The avalanche is probably the most dangerous rescue situation we face. The other accident condition involves hard frozen snow and exposed boulders, the one promoting rapid acceleration, the other ensuring a sudden and dangerous stop. These were the conditions that starry night with just a flurry of snow, teased by a fresh westerly wind, but above 1500 feet it was as hard as roughcast.

The telephone shattered my armchair detecting. I knew before I picked up the receiver that it most probably meant trouble.

It was an operator on the line.

'Meester MacInnes' – she had a lilting West Highland accent – 'will you accept a reverse charge call from Bridge of Orchy? I think it's an emergency.'

'Yes,' I sighed with resignation. It could just be some friend who had run out of petrol.

'Is that Hamish MacInnes?' I didn't recognise the voice.

'Yes, what can I do for you?'

'There have been two accidents on Beinn Achaladair. One to my friend, Kenneth Dunn, who's fallen and is still up on the west face. Another chap, I don't know his name, is injured in the corrie to the south.'

'Are they badly hurt?'

'I don't know, I ran down for help. The third member of my party stayed with Kenneth.'

This was a common enough situation for us. Often the survivor of a mountain mishap rushes down for help before first establishing the seriousness of the victim's injuries or even if help is required. Neither do they stop to work out exactly where their companion is lying. This, especially at night, can be time-consuming for rescuers.

'We'll be over as quickly as we can,' I told him. 'Stay at the farm and I'll get more information from you when we arrive.'

In those days our call-out procedure wasn't so sophisticated as it is now. I phoned the Clachaig Inn, where the owner, Rory MacDonald, was a team member, as were John Gray and Alec Morrison, two of his employees. On dozens of rescues, customers had been abandoned to serve themselves as Rory and his staff took off on their roles as good Samaritans.

This time, it was John Gray who answered the phone. I told him what I knew and asked him to contact the Elliot brothers while I let the police know.

Making fast time across the long straights of the Moor of Rannoch, as the road was clear of snow, we turned off to bounce up the dirt road leading to Achallader farm. The stocky figure of Duncan Smith, the farmer, was framed in the open door of the farmhouse. As we got out of the car, I could see beyond through the snow flurries the stark outline of the Fortress of Achallader. It was within these now crumbling walls that in 1691 the first Earl of Breadalbane conferred with the Highland chiefs on the pacification of the clans, then in arms for King James. Before the Massacre of Glencoe, a Campbell party spent a night here. Luckily, there were no Campbells in our rescue party that night, because even today, Campbells are still frowned on in this area. That's a long time to hold a grudge, as the Massacre of Glencoe occurred in 1692.

I left the car headlights on as we unloaded our rescue gear. A few minutes later I was speaking to Duncan Smith and Graeme, the climber who had telephoned, when we saw a blood-covered figure staggering through the farmyard gate, a macabre sight, like something out of a horror movie. This was the victim of the other accident, who had got himself down. Despite his gory appearance he had no serious injuries, only multiple lacerations and bruising.

Vehicles started to pour into the yard. John Gray and Alec Morrison arrived, followed by Hugh McColl, a Glencoe farmer and a special constable. Just behind, Denis Barclay, Will Thomson and John Hardie emerged from their vehicles and our local police sergeant, Douglas McCorquodale, drove up in his Land-Rover with a full complement. Out jumped Constable George Cormack, Rory MacDonald of the Clachaig Inn, the two Elliot brothers and Ian Clough, my partner on the winter climbing courses. The rest of the police team were on their way from Oban.

Duncan Smith who knew the hill like the back of his hand, had been piecing together the climber Graeme's description of his fallen friend's position.

'He'll be just about the same place where that man died way back in 1925,' Duncan informed me confidently. 'You won't remember that, but my father found the body. It's across on the middle of the face, on the long scree slopes.' He pointed a finger into the dusk to the right of the castle ruin. 'The snow line's quite high just now, so you shouldn't have too much trouble getting there.'

'Thanks, Duncan. Have you got the searchlight, Willie?'

'Aye, and it's fully charged.'

'Good, we'll probably need it.'

Duncan Smith went on helpfully, 'There are long streaks of scree where the chap'll be lying, Hamish. You should be able to make your way up those between the snow without crampons.'

'I hope we don't need any gear.' It was Alec Morrison who spoke. 'I've bugger-all with me. I didn't think that there would be any snow over here.' Some time before Alec had been a member of the RAF Rescue Team at Leuchars and came to live in Glencoe when he finished his service.

We did a rising traverse from above the railway line and were soon on to large sheets of ice. As Duncan Smith had mentioned, there were scree ribbons fingering down through the ice sheets and edging the shallow gullies. We took to one of these, but after fifty minutes' hard going, realised we were too high. We were going to have to traverse.

Alec Morrison wasn't the only member of the team without crampons who had thought that the rescue was going to be a piece of cake. They were soon in trouble. Those of us who had crampons put them on. With Will Thomson, who helped on our courses, I started to cut steps, Ian Clough taking up the rear, in case anyone got into difficulties.

I heard Willie Elliot's voice somewhere along that crocodile of light.

'This searchlight's a hell of a weight, would anybody like to take a turn?'

'Well, if you're feeling past it, Willie, I'll have a go.' It was Alec Morrison.

Later, Willie told me that instead of getting a lighter burden he found that Alec's rucksack was almost double the weight of the searchlight. Rory MacDonald was carrying the folding stretcher and for once was not sporting the kilt, his normal attire for pub and rescue.

I now realised how high we had climbed, as the face here was riven with narrow icy runnels which proved difficult to cross. The steps which Will and I were cutting had to be well formed for, had someone fallen, it would be akin to descending the Cresta Run without a bob, with the added hazard of a multitude of lethal boulders below. Not a pleasant thought.

John Gray, who regained his balance after a stumble, dropped a large hand torch, which bounded down the face. We gazed at it in silence like astronomers observing a new comet.

'That's one way to snuff it,' Denis Barclay observed dryly. Thereafter we progressed even more carefully.

Alec Morrison put the searchlight on. Previously we had been conserving the battery and now the vivid white beam picked out the injured man, Kenneth Dunn, with his companion Bill Jack, on an island of rock. Kenneth had his rucksack propped up in front of him. I shouted, 'We'll be with you soon.' But it took us about twenty minutes. Kenneth was desperately cold, having been lying out for hours.

With the help of the searchlight we found that he had back and hip injuries and extensive bruising. He was in considerable pain. Carefully lifting him on to the stretcher which Walter Elliot had carried over the last part of the traverse, we secured him inside the casualty bag. Bill Jack told us that Kenneth had fallen at 2400 feet and, after shooting down ice, had smashed into a boulder sixty feet down, which, though stopping him, had caused the damage.

We tied a couple of 200-foot ropes to the stretcher and started down. These were well Vd out to give maximum control and also to prevent stones or lumps of ice hitting stretcher and patient. It was only when we had descended a hundred feet or so that I realised how lucky Kenneth Dunn was, for had he not met his boulder on that rocky island he would have continued several hundred feet and would surely have perished on the rocks.

I was getting worried about these rocks – and the ice.

'What do you think, Ian? It's a bit dodgy for those without crampons.'

The lads were kicking their heels into the icy surface with very little effect.

'They'd better go down one of the scree strips,' Ian Clough replied, shining his headlamp to the right.

'I think so too,' I responded and I shouted instructions accordingly.

The powerful beam of Alec's searchlight picked out the steep verglas-coated rocks. Though not inviting, at least one couldn't fall far in the event of a slip. About eight of the team made their way to this frozen gangway. Those of us with crampons took up the stretcher 'reins' and continued down.

We had been going for some ten minutes when I heard a shout and the searchlight beam spun across the dark curtain above before hurtling down the slope, with Alec Morrison still attached. Alec was the only one remaining with the stretcher party who hadn't crampons. As he was operating the searchlight he didn't want to abandon us and leave us short handed. It was a strange sight to see Alec, followed six feet behind (the length of the flex) by the lamp. The battery was still in the rucksack on his back. He did several cartwheels, eventually coming to a halt 300 feet below, when he hit frozen scree resembling a carrot grater.

In our concern for a fellow rescuer we almost forgot Kenneth and his stretcher, which was also eager to be off. I had to yell to the team to hold it or we'd also lose our patient.

Three of us quickly cramponed down to where Alec lay. We were relieved to find that he wasn't badly hurt, mainly abrasions, but he had injured his back. While we attended his wounds, the stretcher was lowered down to us.

Below I saw a host of lights.

'That must be the Oban Police team,' I said to Ian Clough. I spoke to them on the radio, asking if they had another stretcher. They had, and as it was being carried by Ian McCrae, the gamekeeper and special constable who lives just a mile or so from Achallader farm, I knew it would be with us pretty quick.

Though initially Alec insisted on painfully hobbling down, he soon succumbed to the indignity of being carried when Ian and the stretcher arrived. We brought both men down to the farm. The lower slopes of the mountain, which we had avoided coming up on our rising traverse, proved to be like an angled skating rink, sheathed in wide expanses of ice, and made slicker by a thaw which had by now set in. Both casualties were taken by ambulance to the local doctor at Dalmally and then to Oban hospital.

I have always found it a point of interest when thinking of this rescue that Kenneth Dunn was found very close to the location of the 1925 accident.

That early rescue occurred at a time when there were no official rescue facilities in the Scottish Highlands, and psychic assistance was volunteered in the form of 'magic writing', which may or may not have given clues to where the missing climber lay.

A Spirited Correspondence

I have been interested in the mystery of the Ben Achaladair letters for over twenty years. Every time I go on a rescue in that area my thoughts take me back and I am forced to believe that there are some happenings on earth which, at the present time, have no logical explanation. I knew several of the people who took part in the search and have spoken with them at length about this strange affair.

To begin, we go back in time to 1925. It was a cold Sunday morning on 22 March. The time, 5.30 a.m. when Douglas Ewen, Archibald MacLay Thomson and Alexander Lawson Henderson left Inveroran Inn, an old droving stance, to walk to Beinn Achaladair.

The high tops were still in winter condition and there was a crisp clear frost but none of the party had knowledge of snow and ice climbing. Thirty-year-old Alex Henderson was the most experienced of the group, having made some ascents on the continent.

In 1925 the A82 highway across the Moor of Rannoch,

which links Fort William and the West with Glasgow, had still to be built. They took the old road as far as Loch Tulla, then followed the loch edge and crossed the Water of Tulla at a ford opposite Achallader farm.

The north-west face of the mountain rose above them as they crossed the railway line. It was 7.30 a.m.

To a mountaineer this aspect of Ben Achaladair presents no great difficulty, being an almost uniformly angled slope to its summit. The three men chose to ascend a wide snow gully in the centre of the face.

They had been warned that conditions on the mountain could be icy and even lower down on the slopes they had to kick steps. From below, the long treadmill of this slope is foreshortened.

It was 9.30 a.m. before they stopped for breakfast at 2000 feet. Already they were finding the going difficult and, with little thought of the possible consequences, they took an hour over their meal. Alex Henderson, who felt cold, kept stomping about and impatiently got off ten minutes ahead of his companions.

As Douglas and Archie climbed they could see Alex ahead, but at about 11.15 a.m. he slanted leftwards and they lost sight of him behind some ice-coated rocks. But by now they had other problems to occupy their minds. They were experiencing difficulty with hard snow and higher up they found themselves on iced rock. They were so gripped by their predicament that they resolved not to descend by this route.

It was 1.25 p.m. when they emerged on the summit of the mountain. No sign of Alex. At first they were puzzled, then alarmed, and for two hours searched the final slopes, even using a hand siren in the hope of attracting his attention. Archibald Thomson also lowered himself on their climbing rope over a cornice to a ridge below. This was the continuation of Alex's line of ascent. There was no sign, nothing – just a vast angled whiteness interspersed with ice-coated rock.

The two men were baffled by the disappearance of their friend and decided to head for the col between Achaladair and the adjoining peak, Meall Buidhe. They had difficulty climbing to this and had to resort to step cutting on the icy slope. But nowhere could they find any tracks suggesting their friend had come this way. They returned to Achaladair summit at 6.00 p.m. and after ten minutes' deliberation decided to descend to Achallader farm to raise the alarm.

By the time they got down to the north-east corrie it was dusk, but they made a hurried search at the foot of the steep slopes and satisfied themselves that the only marks on the snow had been caused by falling rocks. There were no prints in the floor of the valley, but in the failing light they were not sure if the broken slopes at the head of the big central gully contained tracks or not.

At 7.07 p.m. the light failed and they abandoned the search and continued to Achallader farm.

It was 8.40 p.m. by the time they got down to this place of refuge, and they were fed by Duncan Smith, the father of my late friend, and his wife. The two tired men were asked to spend the night, but they felt that there was a possibility that Alex had somehow crossed over the summit and had perhaps descended to the east towards Tyndrum.

They left Achallader at 10.35 p.m. and walked the ten miles to the Tyndrum Hotel. It was now 3.45 a.m. on the Monday morning. There was no sign of Alex. Both men were shattered, having traversed forty-four miles in just over twenty-two hours, some of that up and down the steep slopes of Beinn Achaladair.

Robert Stewart was the hotel owner at the time and he organised a search party which set off by mid-morning. In those days the arrangement for rescues was to recruit shepherds, gillies and casual climbers locally, and alert the Scottish Mountaineering Club, who would sally forth with all expediency from Glasgow or Edinburgh or indeed from both cities.

Robert Stewart had sent the club a telegram that morning but it was Wednesday evening before it was found in the Scottish Mountaineering Clubrooms in Glasgow. It had been accepted on the Monday by the charwoman who hadn't thought it was necessary to inform the club secretary! That evening the club's topic was a paper on the installation of a mountain indicator on the summit of Lochnagar. The account of this operation by the Cairngorm Club was read by the Honorary President, J. A. Parker. The situation was reminiscent of Drake's game of bowls with the Spanish Armada

115

looming over the horizon. The audience knew of the urgent plea for help at the start of the meeting and as soon as the paper was concluded the president put the matter to the members. It was resolved that a party should set out for Tyndrum immediately. With this rescue party was Alexander Harrison, the present Honorary President. Despite the telegram which went astray, several Scottish Mountaineering Club members in the area were already helping in the search. These were J. H. Bell, A. J. Rusk and E. C. Thomson, names renowned in Scottish mountaineering circles. Frank Smythe, the well-known mountaineer and writer who had been climbing with Dr Bell, had to return south and couldn't take part.

Throughout the Thursday a fifteen-mile radius round the mountain was combed, but without success. The weather had deteriorated with driving rain below and snow above. While police, gillies and other volunteers scoured the lower slopes, the SMC members concentrated their efforts on the more precipitous parts of the mountain, where they thought it more likely that Henderson had come to grief. They concluded that he could have reached the summit at least half an hour ahead of his two companions. It was just possible that they had missed his prints, or that he had kept to harder snow, where his tracks had not stood out, especially in the fading light. With this in mind they felt that the missing man could be anywhere in a wide area, even in Glen Lyon.

On the Monday, eight days after Henderson's disappearance, a set of old prints had been found lower down by some of the local searchers, but these had run out in treacherous ground where the rescuers themselves were exposed to considerable danger.

That day, when the rescuers were on the hill, a strange letter arrived in the post at the hotel. It was addressed to Mr Garret. The hotelier, Robert Stewart, decided it must be meant for a Mr Garrick, who was an experienced Glasgow-based mountaineer in charge of one of the search groups. The letter ran thus:

Dear Sir,
This is going to be a difficult letter to write, and beyond making use of the information it may give, I would ask you to

be so good as to keep it to yourself as far as possible. A friend and myself have, within the last three months, received startling proof of the accuracy of the information regarding unknown people, which we have received from a supernatural agency. I cannot go into details of these now – it would serve no purpose . . .

Yesterday (Tuesday, 24th) it occurred to us that we might be able to get useful information as to the whereabouts of the lost Mr Henderson and at 12.00 noon we approached the usual source of our information, and requested that a 'scout' be sent out to get any information possible. In the evening about 6.30 p.m. we asked for news and the undernoted is verbatim:

The answer is slow in coming, but our messenger now reports that it is raining, and one, I think his name is Cameron, is heading towards the col, where the man is lying. The snow is deep here perhaps twenty feet and it may be that Cameron is not sure of his feet and we cannot influence him sufficiently; it may be I say three, some six weeks ere he be found. Jim says he is warm yet . . .

Some time later: Where may he be found? Can no directions be given?

Such information as I have is scant, but news is that he is warm, and we are not led to think that he is asleep.

What do you say of Death?

There is no Death.

Where is he?

He has not yet passed, but his needs are worldly. It is a col. Ask one, I think his name is Cameron, where he was at 4 o'clock today. They are still searching, and we are trying to help!

Now we do not know a single member of the search party, but should there amongst them be one of the name of Cameron, that would be one point correct, indicating an intelligence of some kind behind our information. I would say that in all probability the whole information as to location of the spot for which you are searching is correct, and that the information should not be treated lightly. Neither my friend or myself are spiritualists, but interested in investigating phenomena we do not pretend to understand. In view of the nature of the information we feel conscience-bound to pass it on – it can do no harm and may be useful.

The only signature was 'Anxious to Help'.

Though most of the club members were sceptical about the weird letter, there indeed was a Mr Cameron in the search party and he had been on the col at 4.00 p.m. on the 24th. Also, it had been raining (a not uncommon phenomenon in this part of the world). It is understandable, however, that the letter wasn't treated very seriously by those hard-bitten mountaineers.

The search continued and a large-scale operation was planned for the weekend as the weather seemed to be improving. Some thirty quarry workers were taking part, travelling from nearby Ballachulish slate quarries by bus. John Kennedy was one of these, and his son, Archie, still lives in the village. Gillies, police and shepherds all turned out in force; the shepherds with their dogs hoped that the collies could locate Henderson if he should be buried under the snow. Some thirty years later I was also to use my dog to find a buried avalanche victim only a short distance away in Glencoe, but was soon to realise that dogs have to be specifically trained for this work, especially for locating bodies. As a direct result, I later started the Search and Rescue Dog Association.

The climbers in the 1925 operation felt that there was little hope of finding Henderson until a thaw, for on the 25th eighteen inches of snow fell, which they rightly concluded must have effectively covered the body, unless he was lying on a windswept slope.

The weekend search was to no avail, although many pinned hope on the dogs. By now considerable public interest had been aroused and on Sunday 29 March an aeroplane from Renfrew airport circled low over the mountain, where over seventy men could be seen sweeping the slopes and corries, but they saw no sign of Henderson. In fact it later transpired that several of the search party had passed close to the fallen climber, but hadn't spotted him due to the snow cover.

Meanwhile, Anxious to Help had become a diligent correspondent. Another undated letter arrived for 'Mr

Garret', offering the following information from the super-natural:

My news is but little, for the 'scout' is not yet returned. You ask me many questions, and these I will attempt to answer. The loch mentioned is not so much a loch as a widening in the Water of Tulla, and some miles from the Loch Tulla at Achallader House, and the ruins of the old castle of the same name. This is Ford.

We did not know of a place named Ford's whereabouts, and had asked for particulars.

From here, if they follow the valley, some say corrie, to its source, and at altitude 3060 feet, they will get as near as I can tell you at present. Today many have passed fairly near, but only a few are out, and there is no sign of a thaw.

We asked for a sketch of the place, but were informed that the 'scout' was with the searcher, one McLaren. You will know if such a person was out, and accept it, if so, as further proof of a direct intelligence.

Still Anxious to Help

Captain McLaren was a well-known climber and actively engaged in the search operation, and curiously it was he who opened this second letter addressed to Mr Garret. Hard upon it, another letter arrived, dated 2 April, and addressed this time to Mr Stewart, the hotelkeeper, at Tyndrum:

Further to my letter of Yesterday addressed to 'Mr Garret', the following, together with the rough sketch, is sent from our source of information and for what they may be worth. Neither any friend or myself is acquainted with the locality, and do not know from which side of the paper the sketch is to be read; but to those on the spot it should be evident if the sketch corresponds to the definite places named on it – we got two separate sketches drawn and they seem to be similar. They are reputed to have been drawn for us by the 'scout' sent to the spot, and the following is his information asked by us for further directions:

Leave Loch Tulla and go along the road until you come to Ford, which lies between the castle and the big house, and go up the corrie. You go east and climb up the corrie on your right hand.

119

Asked if nothing could be done, we were told that the only hope was a thaw – for recovery of the body.

My friend and myself would give our names but in view of the publicity the accident has occasioned we prefer not to do so. My friend knows you personally, Mr Stewart, and I am therefore addressing this to you as likely to be able to make use of the information should it be worth anything.

Anxious to Help

The 'spiritual' sketch showed Loch Tulla, Achallader farm and the castle, but the ford is marked in the wrong spot.

The next letter was dated 3 April.

Further to my letter of yesterday the following information, since received, is sent for what it is worth.

There is little to report; we have found a definite aid to the climbers. It is in the shape of a tin box and many . . . (interrupted)

Has our letter to Garret been received and opened?

Yes, it has been opened by one of the name Mak Lairen, but to the box, some say tin, well, this they will find not one hundred yards from the spot.

But we cannot say will any of the climbers associate the box, some say tin, with the man you mention.

Can the tin be seen?

The tin is quite visible, though snow is falling.

Where exactly is it?

It is near the corrie Achallader, and if they are quick they will find it. A strange message reaches me, and this I will repeat on verification.

Later.

The message is small account; it says the box is empty save for a small bit of linen – the contents of the box is linen and is stiff with batter.

Asked for further directions.

The stream of the corrie is starting at Ford. Yes, you follow the corrie, or some say coire, and it goes to the bogland at altitude already mentioned – 3060 feet.

Yes, it is a burn, though the word is new to me.

I regret my gernadion [messenger] is no longer here, but from the report delivered the news was on climbing the corrie, or I believe korrie, I noticed a box I think he called it, and in it a cloot (I think it is a cloot with a k sound) of linen. This, I am afraid, is the extent of the message, which I will repeat in one particular. The word of the gernadion is in Scots and represents box-mullie.

What is a mullie?

The error is mine — I am sorry my Scots is poor, but it is new to me. The gernadion spoke of the box or a tin as a mull-lie, a diminutive of mull — that is a little mull.

This is all for the present, but he will return with more news and I fear more Hieland jawbreakers.

Later.

There is little more to report, but this may interest you. Tomorrow no search will take place and all trace of the mullie — I use advisedly the word of the messenger — will, I fear, be lost. This, though, I say. To climb the corrie is easy — it is commonly used by — help me with this — ghillies — pronounced ghilly, a species of gamekeeper, from (locally known as) the Big House, I believe Achallader House, near Ford. This route adhered to will prove the great help. The snow still falls increasingly, and I fear that many clues already known to the helpers will be obliterated. One thing remains that it is at about altitudes about 3060 feet that the find will be made when they do, weeks likely from now.

This is sent with the hope it might be useful — in any case no harm could be done by trying to verify it — one route is as good as another when looking for something where no clue already exists.

Anxious to Help

The next letter addressed to Mr Stewart was dated 6 April 1925.

Dear Sir,

I am sorry we have much to give you since my last, but it may be of interest — especially to the 'speculators'!

Saturday, 3.00 p.m.

I say they have your letters, and whilst laughing in their faces I should say it is not in their hearts — they say what is this, who is this? Yet do they say they know something of the affair. Today, but not yesterday, a large force is working and two men are going in the true line of search.

Who are they?

That I fear me is all I can say until the return of the gernadion.

[Captain McLaren and a fellow rescuer were, at the time indicated, heading in the right direction.]

Saturday, 9.00 p.m.

The gernadion is not yet with us. I regret to say the box, or as we have said, the mullie, has not been seen, nor can I wonder. My last advice is take the corrie at Achallader House, which is to say ford, and at altitude given, and to the north you should encounter your object. There is a dark stone ridge – I forget the technical name – at or near the spot.

Is the ridge covered with snow?

Well, it is as though the snow had covered up the middle part without covering the top or the bottom. It is visible.

This last in answer to a question I forget what.

To the searchers I say, walk warily for it is deep.

Is there a precipice?

Yes it is a precipice – I could think only of cliff, and that was not the word. I think Mak Lairen said Heugh or Kleugh.

Has he been near the spot?

Yes, and Captain McLaren several times. [This was verified by McLaren.]

11.00 p.m.

The gernadion has returned. Here is the report. Much talk at Inveroran, and much talk at Tyndrum. They are speculating as to who the comrades are, (ourselves I suppose). They say they too have a definite clue. But I do not believe them as they were too far north. Tomorrow if weather permits, a still greater search will be made. Two of the company believe your good faith – one is called Walker. That concludes my report.

Will the information about the ridge be any good as a further report?

No, I cannot say it will help any more than what I have already written.

Have they got the rough map I sent?

Yes, and they say it is the copy of a map.

Can they make anything of it?

Yes, it is quite intelligible to them. Ford is well known to them.

On the back of the map there was reverse drawing. It almost looked as if it had been drawn on carbon paper. Considerable confusion was caused in attempting to interpret this on the wrong side, for the rescuers at first thought it to be an independent map.

Monday, 4.00 p.m.

My sole news is that owing to bad weather the large company did not materialise and no search of the high ground was possible. The letters (Ours I suppose) have much comment and some heed is now being paid. Stewart says, 'I know no one in Peterhead.'

We might only remark that the sketch we sent was not a copy of a map if such a criticism has actually been made. It was sent in good faith by us as we got it and for what it was worth. The only ford we knew was at the far end of Loch Awe, and we could not connect Achallader with that direction – hence the questions and answers regarding it. We have failed to see any news in the *Herald* since Friday of the search, and all our information we have got from the unusual source originally indicated. We may say that a copy of the *Oban Times* came into our hands on Saturday (of the previous week), and we got a number of particulars of which we had been unaware – such as that the missing man had parted from his friends apparently after a considerable climb had been made. This would indicate that those on the spot must be aware of the original route taken at the start of the climb – this we were not aware of.

Still Anxious to Help

The search was rewarded by success on Sunday 13 April. A considerable thaw had now taken place exactly three weeks after Henderson went missing. Duncan Smith found the body lying face down in a small depression almost exactly where it had been indicated on the 'spiritual' map, and at the altitude given – 3060 feet. Alexander Henderson was lying most probably in the position in which he had come to rest, with both arms in front of his face as if to protect it. The toes of his boots were still pressed into the snow as if they had been arresting his fall, but he most likely came to rest on this easier ground through colliding with a frozen rock, which was supporting him between his legs. He had no broken bones, but there was a large gash on his forehead, two of his upper teeth were missing also his lower front teeth. Later his ice axe was found 150 feet higher and this seems to indicate that he fell from the steeper rocks above, made highly treacherous with ice. Henderson's body was carried down to Achallader farm, then to Bridge of Orchy church before he was buried in his home town of Cupar.

Though Duncan Smith denied that he obtained any help from the sketch map and the letters, indeed maintained that the information misled him, the fact remains that he did find Henderson at the exact point indicated on the 'spiritual' map.

Regarding the other 'clues', the box or tin or 'mullie' was never found, though in Henderson's rucksack, which he was still wearing, a broken vacuum flask protruded through the canvas. Some said this could have been the object mentioned by the gernadion, others thought it could have been a tin with a linen-backed map inside. A cloot is an old Scots word for a pudding cloth. And as for the mullie, that's a diminutive of mull, which, as well as a promontary, can also mean a snuff box.

There was considerable interest as to the source of these strange letters and a reporter from the *Dundee Advertiser* succeeded in tracking down the writer if not the source. The trail led to one Mr Norman MacDiarmid at Buchan Ness Lodge at Boddam in Aberdeenshire which at one time had been a shooting box for the Earls of Aberdeen. He was thirty-eight years old, born in the West of Scotland, educated in Glasgow, and a man of private means. He contributed articles on natural history to magazines. Though Norman MacDiarmid would admit to no part of the letter writing, a statement was obtained from a close friend of his. The account of his friend, who wished to remain anonymous, is as follows:

> Altogether there were six of us gathered together in my house – a friend, my wife, my daughter, myself and two others. The medium and writer of the messages was my friend, who has previously had most startling messages sent in this way. He simply sits down with a paper on his knee and a pencil in hand, which commences to write backwards.

The written matter has the appearance of what might appear on blotting paper after it had been used to dry the ink of a communication, and has to be read by means of a mirror.

On this evening my friends and the others were sitting in the room chatting and joking, and while we were thus engaged his hand began to write. Previously, when in his own home, he had got a sketch drawn by this method, but up to then he had not been able to interpret its significance. The words came through slowly, and gradually the story unfolded itself. We immediately saw that we were getting information with regard to the Argyllshire mystery. The message indicated that we would be guided by a 'mullie' or tin, in which would be a linen 'clout', and that although snow was still falling at the moment, the tin would still be visible.

Interspersed through the message came most irrelevant matter, some of it silly stuff, but this we had just to sift out. I can vouch for the fact that the whole thing was genuine. I was a bit sceptical up to that time, but I am now convinced, although spiritualism has absolutely nothing to do with it. The whole thing came through without any inquiry being made about the Argyllshire affair, and when we were discussing other matters.

There was nothing of the nature of a seance about the meeting, which was purely a social affair in my own sitting-room. As a matter of fact, I was pottering about with my wireless set at the time.

It was apparent that Norman MacDiarmid had a gift before this incident. He and some of his friends had held seances for entertainment. On such occasions he would suddenly commence to write backwards at great speed. One such seance had uncanny accuracy. MacDiarmid's hand had drawn two cars, one large, one small. The small car had the word 'Me' beside it and underneath the name and address of someone in Musselburgh. Next day they were all shocked to read that a youth of that name and address had been killed in a road accident in Musselburgh about the time Norman had drawn his sketch.

I'm sceptical about spiritual assistance in searching for missing persons, and know of several instances where it was tried unsuccessfully. However, the Beinn Achaladair incident does make one think twice about ESP and it appears that the information volunteered had a degree of accuracy. At the time it must be said that members of the Scottish Mountaineering Club were suspicious of the letters, and George Sang wrote an article debunking them in the *Scottish Mountaineering Club Journal*; but even he had grudgingly to admit that Henderson's body was found where it was shown on the sketch and at the precise altitude.

Perhaps we should allow Sir Arthur Conan Doyle, who had an abiding interest in spiritualism, to have the last words on the matter:

> I would say a word as to the Achallader case, which is an extremely instructive one. It is perfectly clear that some one or something brought information to Mr Norman MacDiarmid as to the position of the missing man. That is certain and undeniable. Even names of the search party were given. Now, who was it who brought that information? There are two possibilities. It may have been an unconscious extension of Mr MacDiarmid's own personality. This is an explanation which should never be lost sight of. We are spirits here and now, though grievously held down by matter. What a spirit can do we can do if we get loose. I am just as sure that the explanation of many Mediumistic phenomena lies in this direction as I am that there is a large residue which could only come from external intelligent beings.
>
> Let us, however, exhaust this possibility. It means that the medium's spirit went forth exploring and brought back information. But we have the evidence that the medium was perfectly normal at the time. We should have expected trance had his soul really left the body untenanted. Then, again, this strange messenger did not know Scotch. He had to ask for information from the medium. Is this consistent with the idea that he was actually part of the medium? Finally, he used some strange words which Mr MacDiarmid (who courteously answered my enquiries at the time) could not explain. I think that these words cast some light upon who this helpful spiritual being may have been.

The first word was 'gernadion', used evidently in the sense of a messenger, an inferior messenger, apparently, who was sent out by some superior control. Upon Mr MacDiarmid asking what language 'gernadion' was, the answer was 'Eschadoc'. Now Eschadoc in Greek signifies 'beyond the limits of humanity' and gernadion is connected with a Greek root which gives the idea of one who is bearing something. The latter may be obscure, but the former is perfectly clear. It was while discussing the incident with Mr H. A. Vachell, the famous novelist, that this discovery was suggested by him. It would seem then, that the main control is a Greek – probably an ancient Greek who retains some memory of his old Speech. It would certainly be interesting to know what knowledge Mr MacDiarmid has of Greek, but undoubtedly in his normal state he was not aware of the derivation of these words.

This fact disposes also of the possibility that the messenger was actually the spirit of the lost traveller. The only supposition which covers the case seems to me to be that Mr MacDiarmid's control or guardian spirit is a Greek, that he interested himself in the case of the traveller, that he had messengers at his beck, that he sent them forth, and that he then conveyed the result to the brain and the hand of the medium. If there is any better explanation which does not ignore the facts I should be glad to hear of it.

7

WINDY MOUNTAIN EPIC

The following story is of two young men who, with hindsight, could be accused of acting foolishly and of not observing the basic rules of mountain safety. It is always easy to be wise after the event and there is always a battery of armchair experts ready to point the accusing finger. However, we all make mistakes, especially when young and in the mountains, where often experience is gained through errors. Sometimes these are minor and go into one's memory bank for future use, occasionally they have far-reaching consequences, as they did with Hugh Herr and Jeff Batzer. They will have to live with their mistake for the rest of their lives.

A friend of mine, Paul Ross, was a member of the rescue team involved in this incident, and he was also one of the principal actors in the chapter, 'No Head for Heights'.

Alison Osius worked for Paul in his mountaineering school as a climbing instructor and she knew many of the rescuers as well as the two rescued men. Paul suggested to me that she could write an unbiased report of what was a very controversial incident.

ALISON OSIUS

Thirty feet up a rock wall, nineteen-year-old Hugh Herr presses hard with the three fingertips he has fitted on to a quarter-inch quartzite edge, and reaches right to pinch a sloping pebble. He thrusts his upper lip out in ferocious concentration, then swiftly moves his feet up on to two crystals jutting out like small thorns. He slaps left to palm a dent in the rock.

His last piece of protection is below his feet: if he falls, he would drop in a 'winger' of at least ten feet before his rope pulled taut. His left hand crosses over to a three-quarter-inch hold, his right to one bigger yet, and he cruises to a ledge.

With an exultant whoop, Huey ties himself to metal wedges he inserts into the rock, the climb over: a new 5.12, virtually the top level in rock climbing, in the Shawangunks, New York. Such ratings depend on strenuousness and the size of the holds, regardless of the route's length. Huey, his face tense with excitement, brings three other climbing experts up the route one by one; they all take falls but eventually join him. A fourth, strength spent, gives up halfway.

Huey rappels to the ground, his purple-striped pants and multi-coloured Spandex top astonishing against the grey-brown rock. He rests his left foot on his knee, takes an Allen wrench from his pack, inserts it into a hole in the bottom of his artificial limb, and efficiently unscrews the foot. The wood and rubber foot is painted with an amusing parody of a Nike sneaker. The fibreglass leg is blue, with pink polka dots.

He tried to climb this line on the cliff a few years ago, before he lost both his lower legs.

'But I was doing it all wrong then,' he comments, screwing on a different foot, its purple paint slightly peeling. 'It's all in the footwork.'

Before the accident, Huey was called the Boy Wonder, or Baby Huey (after a cartoon character who doesn't know his own strength). He was a competitive gymnast on his high school team and arguably the best rock climber in the east. Today he is called the Bionic Boy and the Mechanical Boy. In March 1982 he had both legs amputated below the knees due to frostbite. Now, on artificial legs, he is climbing better than he was before.

He speaks haltingly of the mountaineering accident, when youthful optimism and misjudgment, things apart from his technical abilities, brought disaster. A volunteer rescuer died in an avalanche; for Huey, months of depression and pain followed.

Fiercely driven before, he became more so after the accident. 'After all the efforts people made to save me, I felt I should make an incredible output to do well,' he said.

Alone, he slipped out of his hospital bed to practise lifting his weight with his fingertips on a window ledge. The first time he tried to climb rock on his artificial legs, he cried because he couldn't stand up. Months of intense practice brought back spirit and superb ability: 'When I knew it was possible to return to where I was before, the thought drove me nuts,' he says now.

'I'd always had this incredible joy climbing. You're totally narrow-minded, zooming your mind into the rock, into the power of your hands, staying calm. Just calculating and going for it.

'I don't think I'll ever think I'm good at climbing. Ever think I've mastered the mental part of it.'

He confesses to being turned on by risk. 'A lot of climbers don't admit that. Placing myself into severe situations forces the best out of me.'

Another Gunks (Shawangunks) regular, Russ Clune, said that when Huey was only fifteen he was not only extraordinarily strong but 'the most balls-out climber I'd ever seen' when risking a long fall, even a 'grounder', otherwise known as a 'crater'.

From Huey's father: 'He is a fierce obsessive. Climbing for him was the greatest therapy in the world. He doesn't want to be the best handicapped climber in the world, though. He wants to be the best climber. Of the *homo sapiens*, period.'

On Friday 22 January 1982 Huey Herr, then aged seventeen, and his friend Jeff Batzer, twenty, both from Lancaster, Pennsylvania, drove north to New Hampshire for a weekend of ice climbing on Mount Washington.

Mount Washington (6288 feet, 1916 metres) is a formidable prospect in winter, its grim list of over a hundred fatalities making it as dangerous as mountains three times its size. The reason for the disproportionate number of accidents is the weather, which is considered as extreme as any on the American continent south of Alaska. Winds average forty-four miles per hour on its summit, where the Mount Washington Observatory frequently gauges wind velocities of over one hundred. In 1934 the observatory clocked a gust of 231 m.p.h., the highest recorded wind speed in the world.

Huey and Jeff awoke at dawn in the Harvard Cabin at the base of Mount Washington, where climbers frequently sleep. They were appropriately equipped for a day out. Each put on long underwear, layers of wool clothing, Gore-tex parkas and outer pants, and mountaineering boots covered by padded Supergaitors.

The summit temperature was 9°F, and high winds and rapid weather changes were expected; it was already 'snowing like crazy', as Jeff put it. Huey and Jeff, carrying a pack with rope, climbing and bivouac gear, were the first of seven climbers to leave the cabin. They told Matt Pierce, the hut caretaker, they intended to make a day trip up Odell Gully, involving about five hundred feet of technical ice climbing, an equal distance of snow hiking, and a descent via the Escape Hatch Gully. The two hiked about three-quarters of a mile to the base of Odell Gully, on the east side of the mountain.

Deciding that the pack and sleeping bag would slow their progress, they elected to carry only technical gear, and left their bivvy gear at the base of Odell Gully, to be reclaimed during the descent.

Huey later recalled moving fast and confidently up the four pitches of ice in Odell. He wanted to solo Odell, and he let the rope trail free behind him, enjoying the concentration required. At the end of each rope length, he would tie himself into ice screw placements to belay Jeff. Neither spoke beyond a few rope commands, nothing unusual for Huey, who is naturally quiet. The two raced up the ice section within an hour and a half, and began to trudge up the dry, loose snow above. The summit was about 1500 feet further. The boys crouched behind a boulder out of the wind.

'You want to try for the summit?' Hugh asked.

'Think we could make it?'

'Well, we could just go a ways,' Hugh suggested.

'We thought we'd sprint to the summit and sprint right back,' Jeff said later. 'It was blowing really hard, but visibility wasn't too bad. It started out fun, really cold and windy, with ice crystallising on our faces.'

The two boys are uncertain at what point they stopped. A Mount Washington Rescue Report compiled later estimates that they turned back when they reached Ball's Crag, less than half a mile from the top. Winds there were blowing at 64 m.p.h., and gusting to 94; the temperature was one degree above zero.

'The weather was just horrendous,' said Huey. 'I said,

"Let's get out of here." I turned back the way I thought we'd come.' Having no map or compass, they tried to use the wind direction to get their bearings. 'I guess it changed,' he said.

In the wind and snow, the two crossed the auto road at least once without knowing it. This cuts a switchback up the mountain's north side.

For a while, they thought they had found a gully they remembered from the approach. Huey started run-stepping down it, elated. Jeff could barely keep up, and kept shouting to Hugh to slow down, in case he were nearing steep ice in the Escape Hatch.

The two were above treeline, and could see nothing of the terrain around them. They had descended the wrong side of the mountain, starting down the north-east ridge into the area known appropriately as the Great Gulf, and were moving down a water drainage run towards the trees.

'I realised for sure we were screwed when the gully just went and went, but going back up would have been death. It was the trees that saved us,' Hugh said.

At first they trudged through a foot of snow, Jeff said, but well into the woods they struggled with snow up to their waists. Small fir trees, their branches interlocking, further slowed the boys' progress. Daylight faded.

Knowing they were lost, the boys dumped their hardware, rope and crampons, and slogged along the west branch of the Peabody River. Hugh broke through the ice, wetting his feet.

They continued to hike until perhaps 1.00 a.m., then found a granite boulder they could use for shelter, and cut spruce branches to lie upon and under. Hugh, exhausted, his clothes soaked and frozen, would cut a few twigs, then sit and stare. Jeff had more strength, and collected most of the branches. Hugh stripped his wet clothes off from the waist down, and put on a pair of Jeff's wool cycling tights and socks, then his own wool pants. That night, they kept fairly warm by hugging each other, and rubbed each other's feet for hours. The next morning, however, the boys could barely get their frozen leather boots back on their feet.

Hugh fell in the stream again the next day, breaking through to his chest this time. The water, two feet beneath the ice, surged over his knees. Gripped by the thought of being pulled under the ice, he shouted for help. Jeff grabbed a tree with one hand, extended his axe towards Hugh and slowly pulled him out.

At about 8.30 a.m. they came to the junction of Madison Gulf Trail and the Osgood Cut-Off; signs pointed towards snow-covered trails to Pinkham Notch, Mount Washington Auto Road, Madison Hut and Great Gulf Trail. Thinking they were saved, 'We just stood there and cried,' Hugh said. Unfamiliar with the area, the two set off towards the Madison Hut, only two and a half miles away. What they did not know was that the Madison Hut is both above the treeline and closed in winter.

'That's what really killed us,' Huey concluded. 'If we'd taken the right trail [towards Pinkham Notch, four and a half miles] we'd have walked right out of there.'

They wasted waning hours and energy flailing up the steep, snow-covered trail, then turned back towards the intersection. Huey fell as they neared the signs, then again a hundred yards further, beside a boulder. This time he did not rise.

The boys crawled under the rock, pulling spruce branches about them again for warmth. When Jeff tried to take off his boots he found that the toes of his two pairs of socks had frozen to his boots. He inserted his ice axe into the boots, and sawed the toes of his socks off. Jeff wrapped his stockinged feet in his parka; Hugh put his mittens on his feet. During the night, temperatures dropped to −17°F, with winds continuing at about 50 m.p.h.

At dawn on Monday, when Jeff tried to pull his first boot on, he found the tongue frozen stiff. He pried both boot tongues open with his ice axe, but then his swollen feet rammed against the frozen clumps of socks inside. He was able to pry the socks out of his right boot with his ice axe, and he and Hugh pulled together as hard as they could to haul the boot on to Jeff's foot.

'I worked on the other boot for two hours,' Jeff said, 'but I couldn't get the frozen sock out.' (Two years later he reached into his old boot and found the wad of wool still there.) He kept elbowing Hugh, saying, 'C'mon, get your boots on.' But Hugh would lean forward, pause, then drop back. 'His boots were horrible,' Jeff said. 'Covered with ice. He was delirious, hardly saying anything.'

'I wasn't delirious,' Hugh countered. 'I was thinking about dying. I didn't have much to say.'

That morning, Hugh said, 'We'd have these contradictory surges: OK, we have to get out of this – then, we're gonna die.' He gave up on his boots and tried to walk with his mittens on his feet. 'But I could only walk ten paces before I'd fall over.'

Jeff mustered his last reserves, and made a desperate effort to hike alone to Pinkham Notch for help. He wore only one boot; he put an overmitt on the other foot. Several times he lost the trail, buried as it was. The blowing snow stuck to the trees and concealed the painted blazes. He found himself crossing his own tracks, reeling back and forth across the same area in search of a blaze. He finally fought his way back to where Hugh lay.

'Hugh, I failed,' he said.

'That's okay,' Hugh said simply.

The two felt their last chance was gone. 'I totally relaxed then and let the cold engulf me,' Hugh said. 'I was completely numb. No pain. No hope. I'd fully accepted it.'

Neither could stand now. They lapsed into long reveries as they lay still under the boulder. 'I was mostly thinking about people, parents, how they're going to react,' said Hugh. 'It was terrible. So sad. Dying young – I felt cheated. I thought about my friends at the Gunks. I thought about all the routes I wasn't going to do there.' Huey was hugging his friend for warmth, their legs overlapping. 'Want to hear something I've never told anyone before? When I was lying there, I had to go to the bathroom and I couldn't move. I thought, I'm going to die anyway, and I just went. On our legs.'

Jeff said, 'I was thinking about my family, the dinner table. Sweet thoughts. Then about letting them down. It was so lonely. I thought about the chance they'd never find us. I thought about my mom, the closest person to me at the time. Then there were two things left. One was the thirst. We were so dehydrated. All I wanted was a drink. The other thing: I was really praying, out loud in front of someone for the first time in my life. And wondering what would happen to me when I went.'

As evening approached, Jeff said, their extreme thirst was far worse than the cold. There was a hole in the middle of the frozen stream near them, but he knew he would break through the ice if he tried to walk on it. He made his way to the edge of the ten-foot wide stream and, using nylon runners, tied his ice axe to the end of a log. Pushing the log out, he was able to dip his axe into the water. The snow on the axe blade absorbed the water like a sponge. He ate the snow, and twice took a share up to Hugh before losing the energy it took to walk the three paces from boulder to stream.

Lying nearly still, they made it through the third night. On Tuesday morning the two knew they would not last another night.

Throughout that morning they spoke little. At about 1.30 Jeff saw a helicopter above them. He crawled out to spread his red parka among the trees, hoping it would be spotted from the air. When the helicopter continued on, he rejoined Hugh, desolate. An hour later they heard rustling in the trees.

'That was when I looked up and saw "the most beautiful girl I'd ever seen!"' said Huey, referring to a quotation later attributed to Jeff by the *National Enquirer*. ('They made that up,' according to Jeff.) 'Know what?' Hugh said with a laugh. 'I can't even remember what she looked like.'

Melissa 'Cam' Bradshaw, an Appalachian Mountain Club employee out snowshoeing on her day off, was north-east of Mount Washington in the area called the Great Gulf when she came upon an odd series of tracks. It was 26 January, the third day of a winter storm in which winds had been blowing over 50 m.p.h. and the temperature had dropped to −20°F. The tracks seemed to stagger, and crossed themselves several times. She began to follow them through the snow. An hour and a quarter later she peered beneath a boulder. Amid snow and cut spruce branches lay two boys, side by side. Their faces were ashen, with sunken eyes and cracked lips. They turned their heads and fixed her with dull gazes.

Cam Bradshaw was unconnected with the search and rescue effort under way on the other side of the mountain. In fact, Matt Pierce, caretaker of the Harvard Cabin, had become concerned when the boys had not returned by nightfall on Saturday, and hiked out to the base of Odell to call for them.

135

Visibility was only fifty to seventy yards even with a headlamp, and the wind was blowing 50 m.p.h.

At 7.00 p.m. Pierce made a radio call to Misha Kirk, on duty at the Appalachian Mountain Club (AMC) Hut in Pinkham Notch, who responded by contacting the New Hampshire Fish and Game Department, the United States Forest Service, and the Mountain Rescue Service in North Conway. It was too dark to start a search that night, so the operation was slated to begin at 6.30 the next morning.

Organisation efforts began immediately. Sergeant Carl T. Carlson of the Fish and Game Department called six officers who would be available with snowmobiles. Bill Kane of North Conway expected ten to fifteen volunteers. Two forest rangers, five volunteers from the AMC cabin and five AMC employees joined the roster.

The next morning, Sunday, Misha Kirk found the abandoned bivouac gear at the base of the Odell headwall. Searchers reasoned that the missing climbers could be injured and stalled anywhere along the 1500-foot Huntington Ravine, from which Odell branches. They set out to search the most probable areas.

Paul Ross, one of Mountain Rescue's three team leaders, described his effort that day. He and several others rode five miles up the Auto Road in a snowcat, then set off and walked a mile further, heading for the Alpine Garden, which they intended to descend into Huntington. 'But visibility was near zero and winds were so bad we were fighting to walk more than searching,' Ross said.

When nothing more had been found by 4.00 p.m., the search was suspended until the next day. The searchers had exhausted many possibilities outside of Odell Gully, but could not search the entire gully because of the severe conditions. With the help of the gear found in the discarded pack, Fish and Game officers identified the missing boys and phoned their parents.

'They could have been anywhere,' Paul Ross commented. 'It's a vast wilderness.'

Only later, when the rescue was several days old, Ross added, did he learn much about the boys he was seeking and their crack climbing reputation.

As Ross's team mate, Mike Hartrich, observed, 'We didn't know anything about them at first except their ages. They were obviously young – it reeked of inexperience. We thought they'd be in Odell or near it. If we had realised how strong they were, we'd have known they were capable of covering the distance they did. It turned out Herr was a very strong climber, and he'd gone up the gully in about an hour.'

He did not guess the two might have pushed on to the summit. 'No one goes to the summit in winter after a technical climb,' Hartrich commented. 'It's a long walk, cold, the terrain is nondescript, and there's not much to see up there in a whiteout. Of the thousand technical ascents from the Huntington side the mountain gets in a winter, probably no more than two parties go to the summit.'

But even if the searchers had known the two had gone towards the summit, they would not have expected them to descend into the Great Gulf.

The following morning, Doug Madara and Steve Larson of the North Conway rescue team climbed up the right side of Odell Gully until they could see the top ridge. 'We could see there was nobody lying there, so we came back down,' Madara said. 'We figured we'd done our job.' He sustained minor frostbite: 'I think almost everybody did.'

Albert Dow and Michael Hartrich, high on the left side of the gully, found an abandoned karabiner and footprints leading up and out of the gully. They decided to continue up and right across the area known as the Alpine Garden, and descend on the Lion's Head Trail below it.

'We were following footprints, and could see where they'd made belays,' Hartrich said. 'You get a lot of traffic there, but we couldn't tell – could have been the boys. It was easier to walk across than try to come down through the rock and snow slopes on the side of Odell. You'd have to rappel, in that kind of wind.' They lost the prints, however, in the blowing snow. The two started down the summer trail on Lion's Head, carefully avoiding potential avalanche slopes. Crossing the winter trail at an elevation of about 4000 feet, they approached treeline.

'We were on a snow slope,' Hartrich continued. 'I glissaded

down and was walking in the woods when all of a sudden I was swimming.'

A two-to-three-foot slab of loose snow had avalanched off the 30°–35° slope. The sliding snow was approximately 70 feet wide and 100 feet long; it moved about 350 feet down the slope, trapping both men.

'I was carried probably a hundred feet – I was pretty much buried,' said Hartrich. 'The last thing I remember was snow piling around my head. I made a fist and beat at the snow, to try and clear an area around my head. If I just sat there it would have hardened up and I wouldn't have been able to move.'

He had last seen Albert Dow a few feet above him to the right. Both men had been dragged through a forest of birch trees and firs; Hartrich remembered feeling several break as he hit them. He was able to reach an arm into his anorak pouch and retrieve the radio to call for help. 'I couldn't move anything else,' he said.

Bill Kane, eight other Mountain Rescue members and two rangers had started up towards the base of the Winter Trail in a Thiokol snowcat to meet Hartrich and Dow. As the minutes passed and the two men did not appear, the group became concerned and Kane tried to make radio contact; thus when Hartrich's voice on the radio shouted for help, the nine Mountain Rescue members fanned out to search immediately while the two rangers took the snowcat and raced to the first-aid cache in Tuckerman Ravine for shovels and avalanche probes.

Four others who had been hiking down from the Harvard Cabin to Pinkham Notch set off to the avalanche site on foot.

Misha Kirk, who was on snowshoes, had contacted Hartrich and Dow by radio on his way to meeting them at the base of Lion's Head. He assumed the two were on the Summer Trail, approaching the Winter Trail. The search began there.

A few minutes later, Joe Gill skied across the Winter Trail and heard Hartrich shouting below. Descending, he felt movement in the snow mass and knew the whole area to be prone to slide again.

Joe Gill began to dig Hartrich out from the centre of the avalanche deposition toe at 2.25. He was joined five minutes later by Kirk and the nine from Mountain Rescue, then the rangers with supplies. The group started the search for Dow with a rapid probing technique known as a coarse probe, down from the top of the gully, checking the deposition debris and any snags, and then they began a fine probe.

They found Dow at 3.15, six feet from where Hartrich had stopped, and attempted to revive him for half an hour. Injuries to his neck and chest showed he had hit a tree.

The four who had been hiking up to the site arrived, to see Dow being taken down in a sled. Albert Dow was pronounced dead on arrival at the North Conway hospital two hours later.

The search resumed on Tuesday with a plan to break the area into grid patterns. An army National Guard helicopter with a crew of four joined the search, lifting off from Pinkham Notch at 10.00 a.m. The boys were still believed to be holed up somewhere in the Huntington Ravine or Lion's Head area.

In trying to enter the ravine the helicopter met extreme turbulence, which forced it to fly 1000–1500 feet above the area being scanned. After an hour it landed to refuel before continuing for another two hours.

It was that day that Cam Bradshaw came across Jeff's muddled footprints and followed them to their source. She gave Jeff and Huey water, raisins, a vest and a wool shirt, and reassured them that she would return with help. Cam rushed off towards the AMC Lodge, passing two hikers whom she sent to the boys by instructing them to follow her footprints. The hikers reached Hugh and Jeff and covered them with sleeping bags. At 3.20 Cam Bradshaw telephoned the AMC to report that the boys were alive.

Within ten minutes the helicopter was launched, and their families and Littleton Hospital in New Hampshire had been notified. Ground crews set off on foot along the Great Gulf Trail.

As the helicopter approached the site one of the two hikers caring for the boys ignited a red flare. The pilot, Captain John Weeden, hovered a hundred yards from the flare where the trees were only about twenty-five feet tall to lower Misha Kirk and another crewman on a forest penetrator hoist, a disk seat protected by metal flanges.

Kirk, a medic, evaluated the boys' condition and their location. Both were hypothermic and frostbitten; Hugh was incoherent, a stretcher patient. The rescue would be hindered by bad weather, rough terrain, fading light and the eighty-foot trees around them. Kirk remained with hot packs to attend the boys while the helicopter returned to Pinkham Notch to refuel for a lengthy hoist extrication.

Rescuers carried Jeff on a Stokes litter to the evacuation site, an awkward process due to the steep terrain and the three feet of fresh snow on the ground. He was hoisted aboard on the forest penetrator at 5.15.

Several ground crews had now arrived to help, but it was decided to hoist Hugh from where he lay rather than carry him to the evacuation site. This plan would be far more difficult to enact, but speed was now vital. It was dark, and all operations were by the light of headlamps and the helicopter searchlight.

Captain Weeden maintained the helicopter's position 110 feet above the site. Walter Lessard controlled the operation from the rear of the craft, lowering the hoist cable to the litter below. As the litter rose, it revolved so that the litter head was below the helicopter runners. Hampered by his gloves, Lessard took them off to straighten the litter, despite the sub-zero temperatures and the paralysing wind caused by the propellor blades.

'It seemed like he was struggling with it for five or ten minutes,' Jeff observed. 'Then it slid in.' It was 5.45. Kirk and the rest of the party below began to hike out towards Pinkham Notch.

The boys arrived at Littleton Hospital at 7.00 p.m., three full days after they were reported missing. Jeff's core temperature was 94°, Huey's, 93°. No one could tell what their temperatures were before they received aid from the hikers.

The mistakes the boys made are easy to identify. Their decision to try for the summit of Mount Washington got them lost when the weather worsened. They had changed their intended route, so that rescuers looked for them in the wrong places. Had they not ditched their bivvy gear, they could have shared it in relative warmth. Although unfamiliar with the area, they carried no map or compass. A trail guide would have told them that the Madison Hut was above treeline and closed for the winter.

A sharp backlash of public and media opinion followed the accident. Martha Herr, Hugh's mother, summed up the reaction: ' "These dumb flatlanders come up and do this and one of our own died for it." It got so we would wonder, can we buy the paper today or will it just depress us?' she said.

The New Hampshire people who were most critical of the incident tended not to be a part of the local Mountain Rescue Service, Albert Dow's team mates.

'Certainly I don't resent them,' Paul Ross of Mountain Rescue said. 'We've all made mistakes. When I was very young, about sixteen or seventeen, I'd go blundering up mountains. Once I had to walk fourteen miles to get home. I never got bloody lost again!'

Michael Hartrich put it another way: 'The boys did things most people wouldn't have done. But they didn't do anything I haven't done. I just didn't do them all at once!'

Hartrich disclaimed credit for his own part in the rescue. 'People say, you're so brave to be out in those conditions. But for an experienced climber they weren't extraordinary. The terrain was not very difficult technically. I don't think any-body felt they were sticking their necks out.

'It was chance that Albert hit a tree. If he'd ended up like I was, one of us might have dug the other out. We'd have brushed ourselves off and laughed about it.'

Sixteen days after his rescue, Huey was transferred to the Presbyterian Medical Center of the University Hospital in Philadelphia. Circulation to his feet continued to be poor, and the tissue was infected.

Nine days after Hugh's transfer, Jeff entered Lancaster General Hospital. Infection was evident and circulation poor in his right hand and left foot.

On Tuesday 2 March Jeff's doctor was compelled to amputate the young man's right thumb and four fingers down to the first joint. Three days later he amputated Jeff's left foot. Jeff also lost the toes on his right foot.

Eight days after Jeff's amputations, about six weeks after the rescue, Hugh's doctor amputated both of the young man's legs six inches below the knee.

As we have seen, Hugh not only returned to climbing, he became better at it than he was before. Half a year after his amputations, he was climbing 5.11, and two years later he was climbing 5.12 more often and more confidently than ever. He maybe the only amputee in the world to refer to his artificial limbs as an advantage: he is lighter now, so that his strength-to-weight ratio has improved. He has five pairs of feet, four of them for climbing different kinds of rock. One pair features pointed toes for crack climbing. Hugh's technical ice climbing too has improved; he uses rigid crampons shortened to about six inches for improved leverage.

He has difficulty walking on rough terrain, and when a trail is snow-covered, he crawls. Climbing steep ice is usually much easier than approaching it. Damaging the tissue on his legs one day can mean he must stay off his feet for three; the same applies to Jeff.

Hugh speaks of college, and perhaps of training to become a prosthetist, building artificial limbs. But for now, he confesses, 'I'd rather get my slide shows and pants business going, and climb.' He makes his living piecemeal: painting houses, sewing climbing gear for Wild Things Alpine Equipment in North Conway and sewing Lycra climbing pants of his own design in wild colours. He gives frequent slide shows to general audiences and handicapped people.

Jeff still lives in Landis Valley, Pennsylvania, and has returned to his job as an apprentice tool-and-die maker, and his other sports pastime, competitive cycling. One year after his accident Jeff competed in a cycling race up Mount Washington. But more important to him now is his religious faith. He speaks to local church groups about what happened to him physically and spiritually during and as a result of his accident, and plans to go to bible college to train for the evangelical ministry.

8

WISE MEN FROM THE EAST

These two rescue stories from Eastern Europe are about the Giant Mountains of Czechoslovakia and the High Tatra of Poland. I know both of these areas and have good friends in their rescue services, men who are kept busy because of the great number of climbers, walkers and skiers who come up to the hills from the heavily populated regions nearby. Like Russia, Czechoslovakia and Poland have professional mountain rescue teams and usually rescue is free, unless it is blatantly obvious that the casualty acted foolishly. I met several of the rescuers involved in the Czech story. Miloš Vrba is an old friend and one of the authorities on snow structure and avalanches in Eastern Europe. He is a quiet man who could pass unnoticed in a pub, but for years he gave dedicated service to those lost in the mountains of Czechoslovakia. He is also a great storyteller.

Death in the Giant Mountains

MILOŠ VRBA
'Attention! Warning by the Mountain Rescue Services: Heavy snow storm conditions in the mountains. Do not leave huts and chalets situated above one thousand metres! Abandon ski tour projects; evacuate downhill runs and ski slopes! All chair-lifts have been stopped.
    'I repeat: Warning by the Mountain Rescue Service . . .'

The weather is invariably atrocious in the Giant Mountains over Christmas. Fine powder snow falls on Christmas Eve

143

and turns soggy on Christmas Day. Then fog sets in and the thermometer doesn't creep to zero till New Year. It's an unpleasant time of low air pressure, with people irritable, quarrelsome and bored.

The weather was no exception in 1959 and it was what sparked off a rescue operation that made a perfunctory few lines in the local newspaper. But for me it was something more. I took part in the rescue. What I experienced during the last two nights of 1959 and the first waking hours of 1960 forced me to ask myself the reasons for what happened. I tried to understand the physical and emotional motives of that poor boy. The official verdict was that he was himself to blame because he had ignored the warning of the Mountain Rescue Service and overestimated his physical capabilities. This was true. However, I also learned some background facts which, while they did not change the cause of the accident, at least enabled me to understand the behaviour of that unfortunate young man called Jan.

The Meadow Chalet is reputedly the largest mountain hotel in Central Europe. At an altitude of 1410 metres (4626 feet) it is situated in the middle of an extensive plateau girdled by summits. However, with the exception of the highest peak in the Giant Mountains, Snezka (1605 metres, 5266 feet), the altitude between the foot and the top of the plateau fluctuates only between fifty and one hundred metres, so that the area is extremely exposed. Storms predominate throughout the year.

In spite of such climatic conditions, people have built houses here since time immemorial. In the first half of the seventeenth century, after the battle of White Mountain near Prague, the persecuted evangelical Protestants found a safe refuge here when leaving the country. The Polish frontier is a short way from the Meadow Chalet. The reason why people choose to build on that windy, foggy and inhospitable plateau is because of the excellent pasture and a constant source of spring water. One tributary of the river Elbe, the White Elbe, has its source in the neighbourhood of Meadow Chalet. It descends as a torrent through the long, sheer avalanche-prone White Elbe Valley. Not far from a spot called Spindler's Mill it joins the Black Elbe for the long journey to the North Sea.

On 30 December 1959 few people skied, though there

144

were over four hundred guests staying at the Meadow Chalet. In spite of dense fog, four young men left the chalet at 9.30 a.m. They were university students spending their Christmas vacation in the mountains. They were fed up, and with good reason. Up until now it had been a week of bad weather, the usual continuous fog and heavy snow. In two days they would be returning without having even seen the place. Only one had visited the Giant Mountains in winter before, the other three boys were beginners. As well as this, Jan, who was one of the group, was extremely clumsy and held back the others who had quickly acquired the basic principles of skiing. That day, after having haggled about what to do, they agreed to attempt a ski tour as far as Spindler's Mill, an ambitious plan for aspiring skiers. It's a hard trip in heavy snow and at the end there's a steep downhill section.

They made it, arriving about noon at Spindler's Mill saturated, after countless falls. What would they do now, they wondered? Soon they got cold. The only thing they could agree on was to go to the snack bar, though they hadn't much money. It seemed as if everybody in Spindler's Mill had the same idea, for it was lunchtime and the snack bar was hopelessly overcrowded. Jan felt self-conscious and uncomfortable, for he was a country boy and his skiing clothes were baggy and makeshift. He didn't feel he fitted in with the confident crowd in the snack bar and he was in a hurry to leave. Not so his three friends.

At about one o'clock Jan's patience ran out. He decided to return to the Meadow Chalet alone.

'Hold on, Jan, we're coming too.' His friends paid their bills and left with him. They walked as far as the main road without a word. There a quarrel developed because Jan wanted to turn left and the three boys to the right, to the valley station of the chair-lift.

'Why to the chair-lift?' Jan asked petulantly.

'That's a stupid question! Upwards by the lift and, afterwards, we ski our same route back.'

'No other possibility,' put in the one who had been to the Giant Mountains before.

'I know another way to reach the Meadow Chalet,' Jan retorted. 'I found it on the map: the White Elbe Valley! It's longer, of course, no chair-lift, no ski-tow. But I'm sure it won't be crowded. I can't bear those crowds on the plateau and all over your route.'

'Don't be silly. Do you want to climb six hundred metres in this snow and fog?'

'Look, the fog's gone!' Jan pointed towards the mountain with his ski pole.

It was true, the fog had disappeared and the ridge above was clearly visible. But at the same time, the temperature must have dropped for the wind was now cold. Snow began to fall and envelop the mud and slush. Black clouds above the summits indicated more snow was coming.

'Don't be crazy, Jan! Come with us. Within three hours it'll be dark and you don't know the way. There's not much daylight just now.'

'Three hours! That's plenty for me! I'll go alone if none of you are up to it. I bet I'll be there before you. You all ski like snails.'

So Jan went off to the left. The others, after some head shaking, turned right and shuffled towards the chair-lift. A long queue had formed but they decided to wait, though it meant hanging about in the now heavier snowfall and cold wind.

Now, at last, Jan felt in a good mood. He whistled like a small boy, looking forward with pleasure to the coming battle with the elements. Here his old clothes didn't matter. Unfortunately, it is often the case that the feeling of elation and satisfaction is of shorter duration than that of depression and disillusion. Fully occupied by his dreams of solo adventure, he didn't notice a group of youths and girls from the university.

He saw them too late to take evasive action round the corner of the post office for they had already spotted him. One of them was Vera. His newly regained composure was shattered. Vera was one of the most popular girls in the student skiing parties that season in the Giant Mountains, and Jan had long nursed a secret and fruitless passion for her. Secret because he did not know how to approach such a goddess. Fruitless because now, as always, she was accompanied by the handsome guitar-playing Vaclav who effortlessly managed to be all the things that Jan was not.

To his surprise, however, Vera and Vaclav and their friends

146

seemed perfectly happy to sweep Jan along with them to drink tea in their hut in the village of St Peter. Flattered and confused, Jan explained that he couldn't stop as he had to get back to the Meadow Chalet before dark.

'Then why are you going this way?'

'I want to explore new country in White Elbe Valley on the way.'

'What? Going all that way alone? It's too far to solo,' one of them warned. 'If you want a tour through a lonely region, why not go the shorter and simpler way through the Long Valley?'

'Where's that?'

'On beyond St Peter. Then it leads direct to the Eagle Owl Hut. You know where that is?'

'Oh, yes. We passed it this morning.'

'Then come with us to have a cup of tea and, afterwards, ski up the Long Valley, and you may meet your friends at Eagle Owl Hut at the top.'

It was snug and friendly in the village. Brew followed brew and Vaclav tuned his guitar for another song when the Mountain Rescue Services Tannoy system resounded through the wooden walls with the advice about worsening snow conditions. *Do not leave huts and chalets above one thousand metres. Abandon ski tour projects.*

'Well, Jan, now you must stay here overnight!' Vera teased him.

'No! No, I'll not stay!'

She turned to the guitarist. 'I'm sure you'll stay, Vaclav.'

Vaclav smiled ironically and plucked a string.

Jan spoke up. 'I'm not scared! On the contrary, I'm glad that a blizzard is brewing; it's to my taste. I'm leaving!'

'Don't be silly, Jan! It's getting dark. Go down to the inn, ring them and tell them you'll be up tomorrow.'

Vaclav's impatient advice was the soundest he would get, but the last person Jan was going to listen to was Vaclav. Watching him and Vera together had fed his self-pity and frustration. Now here was a chance to show he was some-body, somebody who could snap his fingers at warnings, somebody with the guts to risk his life and fight the blizzard. As they all watched him in silence he just wished he had some-thing more stylish to put on than his old threadbare anorak and his leather motorcycle helmet, and that his skis weren't made of ash with beak tips and with two long hazel ski poles.

Perhaps Vera knew that a word from her could have changed Jan's mind, but she was tired of him and thought he was behaving stupidly. However, on an impulse, as he opened the door on to the swirling snow, she grabbed a handful of biscuits and all the sugar lumps left in the food locker and pressed them on him.

'It's a long trip, Jan. You'll be hungry.'

The Meadow Chalet seems to be a world unto itself especially in bad weather, and is almost independent of the outside world. It has its own well, its own power station driven by the water energy of the Elbe stream; it has its own laundry, bakery and various workshops in the cellar. Upstairs that December night 450 young people, mostly university students, made the two dining halls reverberate with their boisterous high spirits. However, three young men, sitting at a table with one vacant chair, would have caught the attention of an attentive observer. They were evidently worried, speaking to each other in low, urgent voices.

'Look, it's gone too far. We must do something!'

'What, for example?'

'For a start, alert the mountain rescue!'

'Wonderful suggestion, but it's too expensive.'

'Why expensive? Nothing's charged for rescuing.'

'Not unless you've been bloody stupid.'

'Well, that's his problem. He would go alone through that White Elbe Valley!'

'Take it easy! It's a long walk. Maybe he rested in some hut on the way . . .'

'Don't talk nonsense. There's no hut in the White Elbe Valley according to the map. He hasn't a torch and it's been dark since four o'clock. Now, it's half-past eight! Also, he doesn't know the way. Something must have happened. I'm worried, very worried and I'm going to tell the rescue service.'

A siren started, a terrible sound, bringing back to many the sleepless and fearful nights of the war; a sound which tells that human life is threatened.

The engineer of the chair-lift was the first one to leave his cottage on the hillside, and he ran down to the station to prepare the lift for the rescue teams.

At the other end of Spindler's Mill an attractive girl hurried out through the garden of her parents' house, buttoning her short fur coat as she ran to the telephone exchange. She had to be at her post as the exchange was operated manually.

The teacher put aside his red pen from correcting a pupil's essay, and reached for the blue ski-trousers and orange anorak of his Mountain Rescue Service uniform.

The waiter stopped gliding through the dining hall, put a tray of full beer glasses on a vacant table and disappeared in the direction of the staff quarters to get his gear.

The joiner shuffling cards in the bar put the pack down beside his glass, pocketed his winnings and left without saying a word to his companions.

The postman awoke from a heavy sleep. It took him a couple of minutes to realise what was wrong, then he sprang out of bed, dressed hurriedly, and grabbed his rescue rucksack from the corner of the bedroom.

The doctor and the druggist, who were playing billiards in the tearoom, looked at each other, silently put their cues in the rack and left the inn. The head waiter didn't say anything. They'd pay later. They had other things to think about right now.

I help my wife run a private hotel for employees of a Prague factory not far from Eagle Owl Hut. So I am well placed for my special snow and avalanche research and for lending a hand with rescues when Otan, our local leader, gives me a call, as he did the night of 30 December 1959. One of the hotel staff, a lad called Honza, is also in the team. I slipped along to his room where he was snoring loudly. I hesitated to wake him as he had had a hectic day. However, he wouldn't forgive me if I didn't and I couldn't go out alone in such a storm.

'Honza, get up!' The snoring was uninterrupted.

'Get up! Quickly!'

'. . . What's the matter?'

'Call-out. We've not much time.'

'To hell with all those idiots! Just before New Year's Eve, just like last year, remember? Avalanche or broken leg?'

'Nothing like that. It's a missing man. Otan's just phoned. It's a young man who left the snack bar in Spindler's Mill about one o'clock for the Meadow Chalet. He didn't arrive.'

'What time's it now?'

'Quarter past ten. We have to check the area both sides of the track from here to Eagle Owl Hut, then as far as Meadow Chalet. We rendezvous with the other groups at 1.00 a.m.'

'Does Otan know where the man might have gone to?'

'Yes. White Elbe Valley. That's Otan's patch. He's taking most of the team there, but he's also sending small groups to check all possible routes from Spindler's Mill to Meadow Chalet.'

Honza dressed and picked up his rucksack.

'Do we need any other gear?'

'Nothing special. I've a Very pistol and flares. You take the searchlight. Come on, Honza, get your finger out, it's half-past ten already.'

As soon as Honza and I slammed the outer door and turned the corner of our hotel, we caught the storm face on. Conversation was out of the question – the din was horrendous. But years of working together in the mountains meant we understood each other perfectly without speech.

The ridge was marked by three-metre-high wooden posts at ten-metre intervals. Some of these hardly protruded above the afternoon snow cover. We quartered each side of the marked route, concentrating on hollows scooped out by the wind around stunted hill-pines. Visibility was good here, for both fog and falling snow had dispersed. The snow had stopped about six o'clock, but the wind was ferocious and seemed to be getting worse.

From time to time we used the searchlight and I fired several white flares to illuminate larger areas and give an indication of our position to the missing man. We knew the hill region between us and Meadow Chalet intimately. I'm sure we would have detected any unusual object among the scattered pines.

After about an hour's thorough searching on our skis, we cut through corrugated hard-packed snowdrifts and reached Eagle Owl Hut. At that time it was Eagle Owl Hut in name only as it had burned down soon after the war and new premises had not yet been built. In place of the once luxurious hotel a shabby canteen and telephone had been installed at this point and simple meals were available, with a couple of emergency beds.

Eagle Owl Hut is at one of the most important and dangerous crossways in the Giant Mountains. The popular ridge route connecting Spindler's Mill with the Meadow Chalet intersects here with the path from the ski villages of St Peter and Pec.

It wasn't until we dropped into the snow hollow where the hut is located that we caught a glimpse of a dim light behind frozen window panes. In our searchlight the ugly barracks of a canteen shone like a fairy cottage dipped in silver. We didn't want to stop and take off our skis; so we knocked on the roof with our ski poles. The canteen keeper came out.

'What's the news?' I asked.

'Nothing.'

'Ring rescue control and tell them we are continuing.'

'Right, boys. Good luck.'

As far as this point the plateau is almost level, but beyond Eagle Owl Hut it rises abruptly towards a saddle between two hills, a notorious funnel for the prevailing north-west winds to attain their greatest velocity.

That night it must have been in excess of 100 k.p.h. as we couldn't breathe or even keep upright. We wrapped scarves over the lower part of our faces and pulled down our goggles. I headed to the edge of Broad Ridge above the Blue Valley. Honza followed using the searchlight from time to time. It was a difficult section.

The black sky suddenly lightened. There was a glare behind us. A rescue group going up the Long Valley must have set off a white illuminator.

A rescue team ascending the Blue Valley from the village of Pec replied with another flare. It was heartening to realise that we were not alone in this snow-filled wilderness. I replied by firing one against the wind to indicate that we were on Broad Ridge.

As our comet-like flare was falling, I saw something strange to the left, quite a way off. I touched Honza with my ski pole and pointed. He understood immediately and without a word we headed for the spot.

That quick decision to abandon the search on the Broad Ridge and investigate a strange object off our search area later caused me sleepless nights. At the moment of our diversion we were the first two rescuers anywhere near Jan, but we had no way of knowing this. Had we continued in our original direction of search we might have found him.

Our diversion was abortive: the strange object was a freight sledge from Meadow Chalet, full of frozen meat. It was almost buried in a snowdrift. The tractor driver hauling the sledge up from Pec was probably caught by the snowstorm in the afternoon and decided to abandon the freight, rating personal safety above punctual delivery.

Having investigated the sledge, we continued searching the area leading to the saddle. I forgot the section on Broad Ridge which we had missed by doing the diversionary search. We reached the saddle. This next section proved to be the worst. We had to lean against the wind like ski-jumpers, otherwise we could not have moved. The prevailing good visibility seemed strange. The light of the summit hut on Snezka looked like a star and we could see the dimly lit windows of Meadow Chalet. Far below across the ridge we recognised Polish towns and villages. Though it had stopped snowing, when we stood still our skis and boots were completely covered by a dense layer of snow crystals drifting in the hurricane close above snow level. It looked like a flying carpet.

Three green flares appeared in the black sky. One o'clock. Time for the rendezvous at Meadow Chalet. We skied down the slope.

For the rest of the night we searched through the White and Devil Meadows. Though there were about fifty of us we didn't find anything.

On 31 December 1959 it was foggy, damp and cold. The wind of the previous night had abated in the early hours to be replaced by fog. By three o'clock in the afternoon it was getting dark and people were preparing to see in the new year. The self-service grocery at Spindler's Mill was chock-a-block with customers. Skiers forced off the slopes by the fog consoled themselves by stocking up with wine for the evening's festivities, while the wives of the rescue team wondered whether they'd be greeting 1960 on their own again that year, as their menfolk were still up in the mountains hunting for the missing skier.

One of the long-suffering wives was standing in the queue at the check-out behind a couple of students wrangling amicably over the rate of sugar consumption in their lodgings. The boy laughingly accused the girl of giving it all away to Jan yesterday, and she had rounded on him saying was she expected to let that ridiculously ill-equipped idiot set out into the blizzard without anything to chew on all the way up to Meadow Chalet.

The village woman could contain herself no longer and broke into their romantic bickering to find out if they knew whether their Jan was the same man that her husband and many others were out looking for. 'They were out all last night and today in the White Elbe Valley.'

There was a pause while the young couple, sobered now, digested her information.

'Why are they searching in White Elbe Valley?' Vaclav asked.

'That's where he told his friends he was going.'

'No, he didn't go that way. He went into Long Valley.'

On the information gleaned from this chance encounter Otan re-briefed the rescue team and we prepared for another new year on the hill.

We had only been skiing for a short time when we caught a glimpse of white flares in the foggy sky somewhere in the direction of Eagle Owl Hut. As we approached we also saw green lights in the fog. This was a signal to meet up. We were annoyed as we had now to descend the steep zig-zag trail. There was quite a large group of rescuers already there. Otan was looking at something in the snow on the steep slope bordering the path. Footprints had been found, leading directly uphill, ignoring the winding path. All the rescue team now followed Otan. The prints were partly covered under a thin layer of fresh snow so that only faint indentations were visible. The covering of fresh snow indicated that they must have been made the day before, just before the snow stopped at about 6.00 p.m. This would fit with the knowledge we now had that Jan had left the St Peter hut at 4.00 p.m. An inexperienced skier without a torch could take at least two hours to reach Eagle Owl Hut. The climb was long and tiresome. After we finally left the wood and reached the open plateau, the footprints disappeared, covered no doubt by the drift in yesterday's storm.

Otan had now to decide what to do. Where had Jan gone? Straight ahead? Left or right? Such crucial questions usually occur during the course of a rescue operation. Further development of the rescue depends on sound psychological reasoning and, sometimes, good or bad luck. Discussion is often impossible because of the severe conditions. The leader must decide on his own which direction the operation will take.

Otan later explained that he remembered the example of the Babes in the Wood. When they lost the way they looked for a light and went in its direction. Jan probably did the same. From the edge of the plateau he would only see the lights of Richter's Chalet because the Eagle Owl canteen, though closer, was hidden in a hollow.

'This way!' Otan pointed with his stick to the right. 'Richter's Chalet. Do a sweep search, check absolutely everything!'

This was a sound decision. Within fifteen minutes we found one of Jan's hazel sticks in a direct line between the last footprints and Richter's Chalet. Jan couldn't be far away. To be without a ski pole is like being minus a leg.

Unfortunately, the stick was the last clue that night. Although we made various sweeps and cross-sweeps, checking every dwarf pine, we didn't find anything. As the night progressed we became depressed and quarrelled about nothing. I'm sure that none of us knew the exact number of line searches we did to Eagle Owl canteen, then down as far as Richter's Chalet, uphill again, downhill again, across, back. Nothing.

The fog turned red.

'Look, a red flare!'

A red flare was the agreed signal to halt the rescue operation.

But why stop it? Who would give such an order? The flare was a long way off and Jan couldn't have gone as far as that.

'It's midnight!' One of our party looked at his wristwatch. 'A New Year is just beginning!'

'I strictly forbade anyone to shoot flares to celebrate tonight.' Otan was very angry.

'They're drunk, Otan,' I said. 'They don't know what they're up to.'

We started to search again across an icy face. We were all silent. I imagined the others shared the same thoughts: millions of people were wishing each other a Happy New Year at that moment. We just got on with the job.

With dawn the fog seeped into the valleys. The dark blue, cloudless sky turned slowly lighter and the snow on the mountains glared like polished silver. Finally, the sun, that eternal wonder, rose and changed the angry dark mountains into an idyllic picture of tranquillity. We returned home depressed.

I took little notice of the toy-like figures emerging from the forest far down the Blue Valley. They were in a long line on the steep snow-covered slopes. It was a rescue team from Pec taking over. Just then I was indifferent to the situation: I had no interest, no sentiment, no emotion. I was spiritually low. I was exhausted.

Bohous, a skilled mountain guide and rescuer, was on the extreme left of that line in the bed of the Blue Stream. They had been detailed to go as far as the so-called Grave, a sheer gorge where the Blue Stream starts. During his long years of rescuing, Bohous had found several victims there. But there was nothing that day, other than fresh fox prints. Bohous was also a dedicated hunter and seeing the fresh spoor awakened primitive instincts. He forgot the search and followed the fox prints. The fox had gone straight uphill towards Broad Ridge. So did Bohous. But the rescue group continued through Blue Valley veering right so that the distance between them widened. Bohous did not even notice this, he was too absorbed. Out of breath and sweating, he felt a satisfaction in his choice of climbing wax. The skis did not slide back one millimetre.

Cresting the steep slope the fox skirted round a stand of

slender pines. It was at that moment that Bohous had his first glimpse of the animal, but it got scent of him and immediately took off as fast as the deep powder allowed.

'Now it's given up its scent,' Bohous thought, disappointed.

'But what's the reason for it coming up here? There's bugger all here. Food? Its an icy desert. I wonder – could it have caught the scent of . . . ?'

Bohous felt the hair on the back of his neck stand up. He took out a cigarette. His hand trembled as he lit it because he felt he was being watched by somebody behind him. The feeling was so strong that he forced himself to turn his head. It was an involuntary action. He didn't want to turn, but was compelled to do so. He knew exactly what he would see.

His eyes locked on a pair of wide open light blue eyes. They stared at each other for a long time. Bohous's living ones full of fear, the dead ones full of horror.

Jan was sitting against a pine trunk. He had his leather helmet on and his face was sheathed in ice which reflected the cold New Year's Day sun. The rest of his body was covered by the snow.

Otan arrived at our hotel one afternoon in early January. It was an unexpected visit. Honza brought coffee and cigarettes and discreetly left the room immediately.

Together we drank coffee and smoked, we didn't talk. However, I felt something important would be said. After a long time Otan asked:

'Are you sick? Your wife told me that you're not right.'

It was true that I didn't feel well, but it wasn't sickness. It was a mental state which had plagued me since New Year's Day when Bohous had found Jan on the Broad Ridge. I just couldn't find my previous peace of mind. The wide-open eyes of the dead man with that transfixed look of horror had made me blame myself for Jan's tragic end. I told Otan about it and he listened in silence.

'I led the search towards the Broad Ridge that first night. I shot a white flare and, seeing a strange object far to the left in front of us, I abandoned the Broad Ridge search. Jan must have seen us, he must have cried out when he saw us moving away. I am sure that he died from despair which was mirrored in his eyes even in death.'

Otan looked steadily at me. 'No, you're wrong, Miloš. The boy died between 7.00 and 8.00 p.m. that first day, due to exhaustion and shock. At least four hours before you reached that area. I received the result of the autopsy today.'

'Are you sure, Otan?' I asked.

'Quite sure, I had guilt pangs like you. I made a mistake, too, during the search the second night. As soon as we lost his footprints near Eagle Owl Hut, I was sure that he went towards Richter's Chalet, because he would have seen the lights. That was basically correct, and finding one of his hazel sticks convinced me. Do you know why we didn't find anything more that night? Because when you go down towards Richter's Chalet, the lights disappear again behind a snow bank. I went back in daylight and saw my mistake. After the boy lost the lights he must have turned left towards Broad Edge where he met his end. I'll have to get to know my mountain again, Miloš. I know nothing.'

This was the longest speech I had ever heard Otan give and he had not finished.

'In the end it was that fox hound, Bohous, who found him, and none of us could have helped him. He was dead before we knew that he was missing.'

In January 1975 Honza Messner perished tragically on the icy mountainside of Snezka attempting to rescue an injured tourist, and Otan Stetka died nine months later, of a heart attack.

The Three-Hundred-Metre Fall

Polish mountaineers have a reputation for incredible toughness. Most of their high-mountain training is done in their native Tatras, a jagged range which they share with Czechoslovakia. Marek Brniak is a mountaineer, journalist and member of a rescue group which has been on many High Tatra rescues. Toughness is not a monopoly of the male climber, however, and in this tale we have a heroine. It is a story set in February 1977.

MAREK BRNIAK

A hostile wind scoured the frozen lake below us. Swaying under huge loads, Jan and I staggered down in a maelstrom of driving snow, our clothing creaking and our beards encrusted in rime.

The great climbing days were at an end. Dim but welcoming lights from the Morskie Oko Refuge loomed ahead, inviting us to come and recharge our emaciated bodies with hot *bigos* and beer. Heads low into the blast, soapflake snow fluffing to our knees; a few more steps and we flung our heavy packs on to the floor of the log hut.

The place was packed and steamy, yet, tired as we were, we immediately sensed something was wrong. There was an unmistakably expectant tension. A shaggy-looking individual sitting at a nearby bench, eating soup with black bread, told us what it was all about.

'Something happened to a couple on Mieguszowiecki, you know. It's Eva and Tomek, they're on the North Face. Last night they were to signal from their bivvy to report progress and that all was well. When there was no signal we assumed that their torch had gone on the blink. But in the morning Eva's boyfriend was getting worried and went to the bottom of the wall. He could see nothing through the snow storm. About an hour ago, some hikers called in here to say that they had heard someone calling for help.' He jerked his thumb in the direction of the warden's quarters at the end of the building. 'The news has been radioed down to the rescue team in Zakopane. They're due any minute.'

I took my place in the beer queue, always a respectable length at this time of day, especially with foul weather clamping in and little prospect of climbing. I glanced round the room again. On the surface everything appeared normal. There were girls in bright anoraks, men in warm climbing clothes, overweight hillwalkers and lean ones, some cheerful, others looking tired out. They were eating, talking, playing cards, reading. Someone was soulfully strumming a guitar. Fire danced in the stoves and the aroma of cooking mingled with the odour of wet greasy wool and the smell of wood smoke. Clothing and sleeping bags were drying, hung from the walls and draped over benches. Candle wax was splattered over the pine tables.

I had a feeling that these people didn't want to accept their misgivings, their fears that an accident could happen to them too. I know only too well that in situations such as this people often mask their true thoughts with boisterousness and an overstrained jollity.

Stawowy, the rescue team leader, appeared and was forming a party of volunteers to back up his own professional men, who hadn't yet arrived. The volunteers were out on the verandah sorting out equipment.

Jan and I had just realised our dream of *bigos* when we heard the deep throb of the rescue team's four-wheel-drive trucks approaching. In a few moments the white pencils of their headlamps swept the refuge and the verandah swarmed with the men of the Blue Cross.

The Blue Cross is the Polish Mountain Rescue emblem. They were an impressive-looking bunch, with neat matching jackets and breeches that gave them an almost military air. Most of them were Górale, the local highlanders, who are tough dedicated men. They take great pride in their profession, feeling that to be a member of the rescue team is a special honour. Their roots run deep in the Tatra rescue service, the association being one of the oldest of its kind in the world. At one time they were volunteers, now they are full-time professionals financed by the state.

Until now the High Tatra had experienced a fine winter, but the previous night the weather had deteriorated rapidly. It was snowing heavily and persistently, as though making up for lost time. Even worse, the *Wistr Halny*, a warm, penetrating snow-melting wind, had accompanied the snowfall. Now a mass of wet soggy snow was poised on the faces, making avalanches a major hazard.

We had retreated from our route not a minute too soon. Had we continued, the chances of finding a safe way down from the summit would have been minimal. But we abandoned our climb in the full realisation that discretion is the better part of valour.

Now in this insulated world of the refuge, sipping our beer in steaming clothes and feeling our frozen feet painfully awaken, we were well aware of what things would be like up on the North Face of Mieguszowiecki, a gargantuan massif looming over a thousand metres above the slate-coloured ice of Morskie Oko Lake. I didn't envy the rescuers their task. Helicopters couldn't fly in this weather and in order to reach the trapped couple they would have to climb a long steep couloir and then traverse along an extended system of galleries and ledges, now swept by avalanches.

We played poker, discussed politics and, inevitably, new routes that had been done recently and new ones to do. It was getting late and the benches at the tables were becoming vacant. The staircase creaked as people were filtering upstairs to get some sleep. The hut was overcrowded and people were having to sleep on the floors of the dormitories, so Jan and I decided to make ourselves comfortable on our benches downstairs.

Just before crawling into our still-damp sleeping bags we went out on to the verandah to see if we could pick out any lights, but the swirling snow prevented us from seeing anything. As we were turning to go inside again and grab some overdue sleep, it cleared for an instant and we could see the torch lights of the rescue party, like remote fireflies, on the opposite side of the lake, still low, stretched out in a vertical column.

'Not making much progress, are they?' Jan said. 'They must be shitting bricks up there tonight – I would!'

As I was lying in my sleeping bag I could hear and feel the wind pounding on the walls. The hut shuddered in the gusts. Every muscle in my body protested after the exertions of our climb, making me fully aware that I was very tired, but, as is often the case when one is shattered, you can't drift off to sleep.

I lit a cigarette and contemplated the difficulty of surviving such a storm as this, the icy fingers of spindrift searching for cold flesh through every minuscule opening in your windproofs, the blast tearing at the two climbers high above, and at the rescuers, consuming their energy and their hopes.

I had never met Eva or Tomek in person. We had heard they were underprepared for such a serious climb. But the mountains act as a catalyst, giving our small climbing fraternity such a sense of unity that I had a twinge of guilt. I should have been out front with the rescue party. Granted, my presence, had I gone, wouldn't have produced any spectacular result, but somehow I couldn't help thinking that way.

Vivid voices and thuds on the steps of the verandah stirred me into wakefulness, for I must have dropped off to sleep at last. It was 3.00 a.m. 'Why the hell are people going out so early?' I asked myself in a daze. 'Isn't the weather ghastly?' I lay for a further couple of minutes snuggling deep into the down. But the realisation that this was the rescue party coming back percolated into my consciousness and my fingers groped for the zip of my sleeping bag.

The rescuers were a sorry sight, veritable snowmen, their faces masks of sorrow and resignation. I got my butane stove going and made them scalding mugs of coffee while they told me their story.

Crossing the open expanse of the frozen lake, the wind had buffeted their large rucksacks like sails. On the boulders of the scree slope beyond the gusts had stabbed at them so that they floundered into snow-covered holes, cursed, but kept going. It was well after 10.00 p.m. before they reached the foot of the couloir.

Jan Gasienica was speaking, an old hand in the rescue team, a big man with the hint of a pot belly. He came from an old Górale family.

'We entered the gully. It's quite easy going for most of the thousand metres, but higher we were fighting through waist-deep snow. I was sure that we were all going to be carried down. The conditions were very unstable.

'When we reached the bottleneck I was out in front. All I could see were the lights of the others below me and the reflection of their helmets. There was a thud. I was petrified. We've all had it, I thought, a bloody avalanche. But it wasn't; it was the wet snow cover settling. I drove a couple of pegs in a rock crack, put karabiners on them, and clipped in the

161

climbing rope before carrying on. I'm used to rescue work, Marek, I'm not a timid bastard, but I must admit that just then my hands were trembling. I felt sweat trickling down my back. I had now almost reached the point where you leave the couloir and start the long traverse across the North Face. I was forcing myself on.'

He paused for a moment, wiped his brow and took another gulp of coffee. 'The snow was up to my armpits. I half climbed, half swam through it. I didn't pray, I just cursed that snow, willing it to stay in place and not avalanche.

'There was a huge cornice at the edge of the gallery; I don't know how I got through it, but I did. I saw rocks very close by. I could almost touch them. Then I felt something like an approaching train just above me. The avalanche swallowed me and I went with it faster and faster. I was in a vortex of snow particles, spinning, rolling and jerking wildly round and round. I felt the powder being rammed down my windpipe, choking me, and at the same time the snow round my neck was trying to strangle me. I was experiencing the horrors of a drowning man. Then there was this God Almighty jerk and the rope hauled me out of it just like a landed fish. I thought my back was broken, for it had taken the full force of me being hauled out of that wet heavy avalanching snow. I realised that I had pissed myself in shock and my clothes were stuffed solid with snow. What the hell did it matter? I thought. I was alive, just happy to be alive . . .'

Jan Gasienica took off his snow-encrusted gaiters.

'Everything was wonderfully calm and my senses were slowly coming back. I heard Kazek calling to all the team members to shout out their names to see if anyone had been swept away. Everybody called, the voices snatched away by the fury of the wind. Thank God, no one was missing.'

The hut was slowly coming back to life with the accompaniment of the early-morning music from the bogs and the creaks and muttering from the upper floor. Then came the familiar banging of pots and tin plates from the kitchen. Now a maid bustled in to kindle the stove, her hair still awry. The rattle of coal being poured into the stove violated the last delightful minutes of that early-morning quiet.

At dawn the rescue party went out again, leaving us in a

state of silent inertia, with the prospect of long hours of waiting. I peered at the world beyond the windows. The snow had stopped, but the wind showed no signs of abating. It howled round the refuge. Visibility was abysmal.

'This is going to be a bloody games day today. It's not fit for dogs out there!' grumbled my partner, jerking his thumb in the general direction of Mieguszowiecki's North Wall. 'I wouldn't give them high odds surviving this lot, Marek. Last night in the gully the rescue team went beyond the call of duty, the risk factor was too high. I know it's courageous, but it's also silly.'

People were playing cards – poker, pontoon, canasta – as if their very existence depended on the outcome. From time to time one or two would give a glance at the window facing the North Wall and look down at their cards again.

Somewhere up there, high on the windswept face, were two helpless people. Were they still alive? Were they still feebly calling for help? Help which couldn't come.

'What about going out for a walk, Jan? I need to stretch my legs,' I suggested. My companion was shuffling a pack of cards. He had joined the poker school about an hour before but it was obvious that he wasn't paying much attention to the game for he had been losing steadily.

'Good idea,' he agreed, 'and a good time to pull out. Take my hand, mate.' He gave the pack to one of the spectators and stood up.

It was warm outside. It always is with the *Halny*, but its strength had lessened somewhat by now. Clouds were rising and we could see the lower white skirts of the mountains. We spotted the rescue party, tiny orange dots, very low in the couloir, moving as if in slow motion. They were coming down.

We hurried towards them and twenty minutes later met them halfway across the lake. Kazek Byrcyn, the volunteer team leader, told us, 'We intended to fix ropes the entire way up the couloir so that we would have a handrail, but it proved impossible.' He looked depressed and exhausted. Indeed they all looked as if they had had enough.

'The couloir is worse than ever, a death alley for avalanches,' he said. 'They come down every few minutes. Also most of the cracks on the rock walls are jammed with snow and ice and you can't get pegs in. I think every one of us has been avalanched at one time or another in that bloody couloir today. It's Russian roulette. We're all soaked to the skin. I've radioed back to base that we can't go on in these conditions. I'm not prepared to expose the team to this sort of danger any longer.'

We stood there, a shabby group on the ice. After Kazek's long speech nobody said anything for a while. It isn't an easy decision, forsaking climbers who still perhaps have a spark of life in them. You feel it's almost like passing a death sentence.

All of a sudden the face came into view. The clouds rolled up in the wind like a great roller blind. The last remnants licked the high ridges and surrounding peaks. The sun burst through in a blaze of harsh winter glory. One of the team members had his binoculars to his eyes and gave a gasp of astonishment. Immediately we all caught sight of a minute black dot spinning through the air. The body seemed to glide over the rocks and snowfields like a feather, over bands and down chimneys. It disappeared in a snow-filled basin, then took off into the air again, crashing down an icefall. It appeared to be going faster as it fell. It ricocheted off the bottom snowfield and came to a halt on the edge of the lake. We stared at it as if mesmerised, then all took off in a wild gallop in its direction.

It was alive. It was Eva. We could hardly believe our eyes. 'So many of you . . . how awfully good you've come . . . Tomek's dead,' she managed to mumble before she passed out.

Within an hour she was under anaesthetic and having her leg pinned in the Zakopane General Hospital, after a hair-raising journey down the hairpins on a snow-choked road.

What actually happened was this: on the brink of unconsciousness, Eva caught hold of a karabiner and accidentally pressed the gate open, which released her from her belay piton and precipitated her over three hundred metres down the face. What is almost as miraculous as her surviving the fall was the fact that we were all there at the bottom to witness it at the very instant the cloud cleared, for she didn't cry out, and could have lain there at the foot of the cliff until the spring thaw.

A few weeks later a helicopter went back to the face, and Tomek's body was winched aboard. He was taken down on this his last journey to the sanctuary of the green flowering valleys. There at the helipad his mother was waiting.

The first crocuses were just blooming.

9

MIDDLE PEAK HOTEL

I first got acquainted with the New Zealand Alps in 1953 and spent two years mainly climbing and prospecting there. South Island is a wonderful place with a unique feeling of freedom.

This story is about an accident on Mount Cook, an enforced stay in a storm close to the summit. The peak was well named Aorangi, the Cloud Piercer, by the Maoris. Indeed clouds regularly envelop it and winds rush in from the Tasman Sea which is only a skip and jump away, to lash its icy flanks.

As a young man I often climbed unroped in the Central Alps on technically easy but exposed ground and was subsequently told off by pundits such as Mick Bowie and Harry Aires, two of New Zealand's great mountain guides. Nowadays such 'rashness' is more accepted as a valuable means of saving precious time on long routes.

Despite my early misdemeanours I am still in close contact with these rugged mountaineers of the antipodes and this tale of Mount Cook was written by Bob Munro, a guide who worked for Alpine Guides and played an important part in this rescue operation. It illustrates the close ties that now exist between the helicopter and the rescue team.

BOB MUNRO

Mark Inglis and Phil Doole flew by ski-plane into Plateau Hut on the eastern flanks of Mount Cook on 15 November 1982 for a quick climb of this mountain during their days off before going back to work on the National Park alpine rescue team.

They actually returned two weeks later after doubling the record for survival above 10,000 feet (3000 metres) in the Southern Alps, amidst the most intense media-generated public interest ever in an incident in the New Zealand mountains.

Inglis was a full-time mountaineer for the National Park after having given up a promising ranger training course to pursue his life in the mountains. Married, with a young daughter, he is small, almost frail-looking, but he had put up enough good climbs and been involved in rescue operations himself that he took over that season as the leader of one of two specialised alpine rescue teams based at Mount Cook.

Phil Doole, a qualified surveyor, was working his first season as a rescue mountaineer. Phil had already shown his capacity for survival in the mountains three years earlier during another alpine drama. An avalanche had claimed the lives of two people in an accident in the Upper Linda Glacier of Mount Cook. Doole and his companion were hurrying down to raise the alarm when his companion fell in a crevasse, the rope jerked tight and Doole was catapulted into the crevasse, breaking his leg and arm. With minimum clothing (the rest had been donated to the survivors of the first accident), he lay for two days in the crevasse and was finally rescued with thirty centimetres of new snow on top of him.

The climb the two had decided on is one of the classics of the New Zealand Alps. Rising in a series of sharp ridges to where it blends with the Caroline Face of Mount Cook, the East Ridge offers a lengthy snow and ice climb until it tops out at the Middle Peak right in the centre of the mile-long summit ridge.

The pair trudged over the Grand Plateau that first afternoon and spent the night in a crevasse at the base of the climb. They were planning a fast ascent and were lightly equipped. They had pile clothing and windproof outer garments but no bivouac sac, sleeping bags or stoves.

They began the climb at 5.00 a.m., finding that early in the season there was still plenty of unconsolidated snow on the ridge and hard ice conditions on the upper part of the face, making the going slow and painstaking. They could see as they climbed that the wind was starting to whip across the summit ridge but figured even if it was strong they would be able to force their way over the top and get quickly below the crest on the western side via Porter Col.

They weren't to know that they were at the beginning of one of the worst summers that region experienced. In fact a very unusual set of circumstances was developing that played the dominant role for the next two weeks in their lives and was part of a global weather imbalance. The Southern Oscillation index, a measurement of the relative strengths between two of the Pacific's most important weather balancing acts – the Australian–Indonesian low and the high-pressure system east of Tahiti – had begun one of its periodic shifts. Pressures rose in the centre of the low system bringing widespread drought in Australia, while the Central Eastern Pacific experienced devastating cyclones. The phenomenon 'El Nino' affected most continents that year except Europe. The normally positioned Pacific high decayed until the pressure imbalance between Tahiti and Darwin was the strongest ever. In New Zealand this meant the establishment of a strong south-west jet stream in the upper air layers that showed unusual persistence.

Doole and Inglis started their climb just as this system was beginning and by 6.00 p.m. when they finally crested the summit ridge of Mount Cook they were caught right in the teeth of it. Mount Cook juts up 12,349 feet (3765 metres) only twenty miles from the Tasman Sea, so any winds from the west are usually speeded up as they pass over this impressive barrier to their path. The East Ridge is ideally sheltered from these winds but there is no respite on the summit ridge itself.

Frozen from belaying each other and unable to make any progress against the wind, they crept into a small crevasse between the middle peak of Mount Cook and Porter Col, the gateway to safety. There is usually a good bergschrund in that area and it's often used as a planned bivouac. A guided party had spent a week in nearly the same spot three years before, trapped by weather, but also equipped with sleeping bags, and they emerged with only minor frostbite.

The bergschrund this year was small, about the size of a single bed – open-ended so that spindrift constantly blew through.

Over the next couple of days they made several attempts to get out, laboriously roping up then realising as they poked their heads out that there was no chance of survival beyond the bergschrund, and reluctantly being forced back inside to the feeling of utter helplessness at not being able to solve their predicament.

In the village concern had been growing since the first evening when they hadn't come on the regular 7.00 p.m. radio schedule at Empress Hut on the western side of Mount Cook, their final goal from the top of the climb.

On the third day of their enforced stay they were obviously in trouble. That day at lower elevations a party of climbers had managed to get out from Gardiner Hut on the lower slopes of Mount Cook up the Hooker Valley, so if Inglis and Doole were in a position to move, that was the day.

As a precaution a park rescue team that had been training on the mountain range above the Mount Cook village was flown out in case it was needed the next day.

Most mountain search and rescue in New Zealand is undertaken by volunteer groups under police supervision but at Mount Cook specialised professional teams have evolved, largely to combat the serious and frequent nature of mountain search and rescues in the area.

While not tall mountains by world standards, the Southern Alps are rugged, heavily glaciated and with often dubious-quality rock. The weather changes rapidly and the storms can be as powerful as those in Patagonia or Antarctica.

Searches at Mount Cook are controlled by the Chief Ranger and usually involved helicopter support, either the air force with Iroquois machines or the local civilian pilot, Ron Small, with his Aerospatiale Squirrel. Small and his helicopter became the central piece in the unfolding drama.

The fact that the rescue received such intense media coverage was largely due to Chief Ranger Bert Youngman. In the highly emotive world of mountain accidents the press is usually kept at bay through irregularly issued reports via the police. At the beginning of this long search local television teams were allowed into the crew room during the operation, but as the waves of new reporters built up this was stopped, although press conferences continued. In fact the presence of the news media in such force and the gathering public interest in the events sometimes overshadowed the rescue itself.

By the Friday morning, day four for Inglis and Doole, the

park team were on full search and rescue standby. This meant that all other work was suspended and they had to be in full climbing kit with everything packed ready to go at a moment's notice. The only problem was that because of the raging storm nobody was going anywhere.

The pattern that was to become so familiar over the next week established itself that day: getting geared up, doing the mental exercise that would enable the mind and brain to be roughly in the same place as the body might find itself being whisked to in this age of rapid helicopter transport. But the team just had to sit there. And sit there, like the runner being called to the blocks but never getting the release of the gun. The nervous tension builds up but is never channelled into action.

On the mountain by this time Inglis and Doole realised that they were past being able to help themselves. Mark Inglis wrote:

'So much spindrift entered our alcove that it would have been very foolish to utilise our body heat to warm our feet. This resulted in the main complication of our stay. In my case, the frostbite started after the second night and was due mainly to excessive sweating during the climb, which drenched my inner boots and my two pairs of dry socks. Limited massage and elevation of our feet was as much as we could do.

'A great deal of our time in the hole was spent lying, completely switched off. Every day we checked outside and each time we were nearly blown to kingdom come! Cold was with us all the time. Though seldom warm we only shivered after moving around, upon going outside or in the middle of the night. I am still convinced that in our situation, doing as little as possible was the best decision. From the first day we rationed food; not consciously – merely from habit. An average day was two biscuits and two or three spoonfuls of drink concentrate. Water was at a premium. Snow in the spare water bottle was melted by body heat under my clothing. This in itself tended to draw a large amount of heat from the body. I weighed 46 kilos (7 stone 3 pounds) on entering hospital, 13 kilos (28 pounds) lighter than normal.'

The weather worsened through Saturday and Sunday. Snow fell to low levels and the Ball Hut Road from Mount

Cook village to the Tasman Glacier lookout was closed because of the avalanche danger.

At Tasman Saddle Hut at the head of the glacier at 7500 feet (2250 metres) the recording anemometer was ripped off its bolts by the wind, landing 50 metres away.

There was the odd brief lull between the rapidly advancing fronts on the Sunday, and cloud had cleared back on the lower part of the East Ridge to enable pilot Ron Small to recce part of the route that the climbers had taken. No sign was seen but the rescuers got a nasty fright when cloud developed suddenly, completely enveloping the helicopter as it was hovering just above the rocks and snow on the ridge. A brief hole in the cloud allowed a narrow escape for the Squirrel's occupants.

During the next two days a widespread weather watch was begun, supplementing the meteorological service in Christchurch and with observers ringing the Mount Cook area, looking for the briefest opening to stage a search attempt.

The daily routine for the searchers involved a flurry of pre-dawn activity followed by tense waiting through first light as this appeared to offer the best time for a respite from the wind and cloud. Then when nothing eventuated, ringing relatives to inform them of the situation and dealing with the ever-growing press corps.

Anything at all could have happened to the two climbers but if they were still alive after nearly a week out, then their only hope would have been the known bergschrund near the Middle Peak.

Arrangements were made to bring Dr Dick Price from Oamaru, 120 kilometres away, if they were found alive. Dr Price is a specialist in mountain medicine and frostbite, with experience of many New Zealand Himalayan expeditions.

By Sunday evening small progress had been made with the cloud lifting on the eastern flanks of the mountain, enough to enable two mountaineers to be landed at the Plateau Hut where they confirmed Inglis' and Doole's intentions from the hut log book.

On Monday 22 November (Day 7) the cloud base had lifted a little and just after 9.00 a.m. Ron Small flew four climbers up the Hooker, hoping to land them on the white ice from where they could struggle up to Gardiner Hut. He actually touched down on bare ice above the hut and as everybody clambered out his forward-speed indicator registered eighty knots! Helicopters have been taking the drudgery and hard work out of alpine rescue for some time now. The Squirrel was showing that it could function at the edge of climbable conditions.

That evening though, the wind briefly relented. Although great orographic banner clouds swirled out in the lee of Mount Cook, the summit ridge became visible for the first time in a week, and the rescue staff at Gardiner Hut reported patches of blue sky above them.

Ron Small was in the air again. Here is the rescue log for that evening:

1914 hrs	HWW [call sign of Small's helicopter] have located one climber, red jacket waving from schrund to NW Porter Col.
1922 hrs	Dr Dick Price on way to Mount Cook.
1932 hrs	HWW – have lost drop bag. Request from Don Bogie to prepare climbing team to drop on lower Empress.
1935 hrs	HWW returns to Park Headquarters.
1940 hrs	Decision made to continue throwing out drop kits and then place four climbers at Empress.
2025 hrs	Successful first drop, second and third.
2049 hrs	Radio Call 'This is Hotel Middle Peak. Mark lost feeling all toes, no food since Wednesday. Phil, two big toes frozen, sched in thirty minutes.'

So they were alive! And still with a sense of humour.

The five toll lines out from the village were immediately jammed by the media and Park Headquarters had great difficulty in getting through to Dr Price, but the huge public interest that had people hanging on to every bulletin was working for the rescuers as well.

Dr Price was whisked by police car to the Oamaru Airport at speeds normally associated with the most dangerous hit-and-run cases. Over the next week repair men thought nothing of driving 300 kilometres to fix broken office equipment at Search Headquarters or oxygen equipment distributors travelling from Dunedin, also 300 kilometres away, with some urgently needed gauges and cylinders.

But those minutes after the news came through that they were alive were hectic at Search and Rescue Headquarters. The first drop bag had been lost over the edge of the bergschrund and new ones hastily prepared as the light rapidly faded. One of the most relaxed people appeared to be Phil Doole's mother. Upon being rung in Wellington to be told that her son was alive, she replied that she always knew he would be and that he was good for a few more days yet, and she didn't want anybody taking any risks on his account!

Rescuer Ken Joyce explained later how they had spotted from the helicopter one person waving from a small berg-schrund below the main Middle Peak bergschrund as Ron worked out how to ride the express train that was the wind pouring over the summit ridge. They tried dangling the drop kit out on a rope but the wind kept trailing it up towards the tail rotor. Next they tried bombing. Ken held the bag out the door and let go on Ron's command. The bag landed near the entrance to the bergschrund, teetered briefly on the edge then rolled off down the slope. Returning with three more kits they tried the same procedure. Ron put just enough bite on his blades to avoid windmilling them past the safety limit and with the engine barely idling they rode an escalator of wind up towards the bergschrund. Ken held the first bag out over the skids and let go when Ron called. The bag plumbed down right on target. Two more shots – two more successes – the last bag landed right on Phil Doole.

So they had been found and supplied with sleeping bags and food but the storm and the wind were back in full force the next morning so there was no hope of rescue. If the wind wouldn't allow a helicopter rescue, then it was going to have to be done on foot. So a plan was prepared in the event that they would have to be lowered off Mount Cook in a stretcher by ground parties. This would involve a lot of manpower, complicated rope work and again some respite from the weather. The prospect of bouncing those frostbitten feet, now susceptible to damage as they re-warmed in the sleeping bags, all the way off the top of Mount Cook, wasn't appealing either. Four alpine guides were brought in to swell the numbers of the rescue teams and a group of volunteers put on standby in Timaru, two and a half hours' drive away.

For Inglis and Doole, as they entered the second week of their stay, their ordeal was in some ways worse than the first. Up to the moment of being found they were engaged in the simple primitive art of survival. Once warm and fed and in radio contact with the base, their horizons broadened and they became concerned about the wider implications. What was going to happen to those frozen lumps at the ends of their legs? Would the rescuers carry things too far and a serious accident occur? Mark's wife Anne spoke briefly on the radio and messages were sent from Phil's family in Wellington.

These messages affected the climbers' morale, bringing in a flood of feelings that had been kept in abeyance during the bitter struggle to stay alive in a hole in the snow at 12,000 feet, lying on a thin mat with feet jammed into the bottoms of packs, as the thermometer dipped to −20°C during that succession of long nights. When rescued Mark had a frost-bitten finger from the constant pressing of the light button on his watch that measured the slow passing of each night.

But the weather that made 1982–83 such a freak season throughout the world, which enhanced the droughts in Africa and Australia and produced hitherto unknown hurricanes in Hawaii, continued in the same pattern; 200-k.p.h. winds from the south-west quarter lashed Mount Cook with rain and snow to low levels.

By now all New Zealand was following the drama via their TV sets and radio news bulletins. But there was so little to report. After two more days radio contact was lost with the pair. Although it was probably just battery failure, the lack of contact increased the anxiety.

By Friday 26 November, four days after they had been found and eleven days since they started climbing, a partial respite on the lower slopes of the mountain allowed the climbing team at Gardiner Hut to be brought out, but that was all. Saturday the 27th was a repeat of all the other days but the forecast was for the south-west jet stream to weaken finally on Monday and be completely clear of the region by Tuesday. Dr Price gave two to four days' grace before any serious medical problems would develop.

The next day Bert Youngman decided to bring in an RNZAF Iroquois helicopter to help in ferrying climbers, as the option of having to do a long stretcher lower was a real possibility. It arrived just after 6.00 p.m., when the weather began another one of those 'race against the dark' evening clearances. The sky was still threatening to the south but the area around the top of Mount Cook began to clear back. So it was decided to establish a group of strong climbers on the Empress Shelf, a snow plateau about 1500 feet (450 metres) below the stranded pair. If the rescue couldn't be effected that night at least rescuers would be able to get up to the pair even in difficult conditions the next day.

Events over the next hour moved swiftly.

Ron Small took off in the Squirrel with a load of rescue personnel. He landed them in fresh knee-deep snow on the Empress Shelf and then flew up to the summit ridge. To Ron the configuration of the snow slope seemed to have changed and he thought the bergschrund had collapsed on its occupants and he could see bodies lying out on the snow. He radioed that he was coming back and could Bert Youngman come out to the helicopter to meet him. The Search Headquarters was under virtual siege at this stage by reporters who sensed that something dramatic had happened.

Just as the Squirrel swung away from whatever had happened at Middle Peak Hotel the Iroquois came in to land at the advance base on the Empress Shelf with the rest of the rescue party. As the pilot put the machine into a hover in preparation for landing, the blades blew up drifts of the new snow. The pilot lost his horizon in the swirling whiteout, the tail plane hit the ground and the helicopter flipped on to its back, the tail plane and rotor hanging over the 1000-foot drop to the lower Empress Shelf.

The park mountaineers burst out of the side of the stricken machine, followed by the Iroquois crew. Apart from some minor injuries no one was hurt. For Ron Small, hovering above, after two weeks of dawn-to-dusk standby and some very difficult mountain flying, this was getting to be the last straw. He had to leave the mystery of the Middle Peak bergschrund and now rescue the Iroquois crew. Daylight was fading fast and a southerly front was sweeping across the

Mackenzie country. It was snowing heavily only twenty-five kilometres away from Mount Cook.

Inside the chill confines of Middle Peak Hotel Phil Doole was trying to keep a record of the passing time. It was the evening of Day 11:

Waiting. Watching mossy threads of spindrift overhead. The light of another dawn spreads into the tunnel. Waiting. Listening. Just the slightest shiver runs across the roof. Silence. Is it really calm outside . . . ?

Stirring. Searching for the transistor radio amongst the clutter. The two RTs are kaput. Station 3ZA has the only steady signal, no surprise – it's a direct line of sight to the transmitter at Kumara, only 145 km [90 miles] north of Mount Cook. Familiar sounds of West Coast breakfast radio. Have a nice day. Sure, anytime. But our isolation is quickly blown away by Morning Report: a wrecked Iroquois lies on the Empress Shelf. What! We trade expletives and wait for the rest . . . thoughts zeroing in on people, mates, lives. Anxious, we want to know more from this noise invading our hole. No more . . .

Meanwhile, another drama was unfolding at Search Headquarters:

To take the pressure of reporters off his back, (they knew that Ron had reported something strange) Bert Youngman sent a member of his staff out the door to the press to say that despite appearances hope was not given up for the climbers. For instance, in cases of severe hypothermia even people who appeared clinically dead had been revived.

A reporter at the back of the group picked up on these words and raced off to ring his office with the dramatic news that after all the struggle the two mountaineers overdue on Mount Cook were 'clinically dead'. Even the news reader who had to read out the bulletin on TV looked dubious as he read the words but the mistake had been made and the news was broadcast around the country. The shaken parents and relatives tried to ring through for verification of the dreadful news but once again the phone lines to the small alpine village went into overload.

Darkness was nearly upon the scene and time had run out for a proper rescue attempt that night. Ron Small managed to make one flight back in after bringing out the Iroquois crew.

Another drop bag went over the side to the entrance of the bergschrund and, unaware of all the drama the premature news of his demise was causing, a figure in a blue jacket strolled out of the cave, picked up the bag and disappeared again. The two bodies that Ron thought he had seen were empty drop bags that the conscientious pair had staked into the snow to mark their exact location.

Monday the 29th just had to be the day. The forecast at 4.00 a.m. indicated the lowest wind speeds yet at 3000 metres. At dawn the team on the Empress Shelf reported that everything above them was clear. They had finally snatched some sleep at 3.00 a.m. after digging snow caves most of the night. They weren't digging just a shelter for themselves but a potential field hospital in case evacuation only got that far before becoming bogged down by the weather. Dr Price was there with a full medical kit including oxygen and a portable defibrillator.

The only problem was that everywhere on the east of the Main Divide there was a thick sheet of low cloud. It hugged the ground around the Mount Cook village and spread far out into the Mackenzie Country. The temperature at Mount Cook was 0°C and then it began to snow, fine above, atrocious below. The forecasters were predicting a break in the clouds but it wasn't appearing. The worst possible scenario was for the rescue to get under way and then for cloud to form around the machines as they were lifting people out. Ron Small had decided that after the previous night's events he needed some support from the people he knew well. Bill Black, the legendary bush pilot from the rugged Fiordland area, came through with his Squirrel and brought with him Rex Dovey who had taught Ron how to fly.

Back to Phil Doole at Middle Peak Hotel:

7.30 a.m. Radio New Zealand news: Middle Peak Hotel has the lead: No mention of the wreck – that's old news. The Chief Ranger outlines today's rescue plan for the nation to digest. Better get ourselves organised, lad. Sounds like this could be it.

I find the overboots which arrived in the last airdrop, last night. Pull them on over cold socks. I read the name – borrowed gear. So was the transistor radio, I find out later.

177

Long laces and lots of hooks, clumsy fingers. Quiet communication between us: some worry, some anticipation of the action. Wonder who'll be on the strop? Laces just tied and we hear the chopper. Gotta go.

Outside it's brilliant. The crisp air wakes a weary, troubled mind. An early-morning glow and the Tasman Sea glittering not so far away. The sun lets me feel warm.

A new RT comes down by rope. Calling Hotel-Whisky-Whisky draws no response; where's the chopper gone? On to the other channel, and it takes Search Control a little while to react. Put it all on hold, fight the worry trying to burst out. Asking the question: 'Who copped it in the crash?' The answer comes unexpectedly from Lisle Irwin, senior ranger, back from vacation: 'Everyone's OK, Phil.' All right then. We're ready for a lift. Don't push it.

By 7.30 a.m. the cloud in the Hooker Valley was still holding a ceiling of 2700 metres and the decision was made to go. It was 3200 metres out over the Tasman riverbed before the two Squirrels broke into sunlight and swung back towards the Hooker. A quick recce flight lowered another radio down to the bergschrund. Soon Phil's strong voice reported that he could be lifted out on his harness but that Mark should be moved in a stretcher.

Ron landed on the shelf and the strop system was set up, first developed by Canadian rescue teams. The helicopter takes off with the rescuer dangling twenty metres below, which enables him to be flown into tight locations with the helicopter hovering above. The sensation of flying this way is not unpleasant. It's similar to parachuting, usually lasts longer and there is no nasty thump at the end. So long as the pilot is doing his job.

The senior mountaineer, Don Bogie, had developed this system at Mount Cook along with Ron Small. It had been in use for two seasons but so far had been tried only with rescuers picking up bodies in dangerous locations. Now it was Bogie's opportunity to try it out on some climbers still very much alive.

Also as an aid for a quick pick-up, Bogie had adapted another Canadian modification of a European compact stretcher. The Bauman bag is a large nylon bag opening its full length with a series of attachment points that join it to the bottom of the helicopter strop. This simple bag can be carried on the rescuer's hip, quickly unpacked, the patient rolled in and attached to the strop with the helicopter hovering above. This way the rescuer doesn't have to detach from the strop and the helicopter spends the minimum time in the hover in a dangerous location.

So, with the cloud boiling up below them, a white wall of southerly snow showers on the horizon and the first sign of clouds already beginning to appear over the Caroline Face just above where Mark and Phil were trapped, they set to work.

Phil Doole again:

Alone, back in our tunnel. Our hole is a mess of gear, empty gas canisters, unused food, and yellow snow. Gathering together the RTs. Leaving everything else behind, even my ice axe, when the chopper returns again.

Smack on the shelf! Don unclips our harnesses and is gone. Alone again for a moment, body tuning to this new locale. Whisto crouches in the snow. A quiet grin from a face dark with stubble: 'Gidday, man.' Dull awareness of activity about the landing pad; proficiency typified by a line of safety pickets leading out to the wreck.

Don Bogie reported later:

We landed on the Empress Shelf and set up the strop, tying each end of the two strands to the fixed bolts underneath the helicopter. I clipped my harness on to the other end and two minutes later was dangling in the −20°C air over the bergschrund. Ron lowered me to the snow right at the entrance. Mark was in a sleeping bag about three metres inside so I asked Ron to give me more rope. I went inside and dragged Mark back to the entrance so that I could work on him in the open. Ron was hovering about fifteen metres above as Phil came out of the cave to help me get Mark into the Bauman rescue bag. I checked all my attachments then the stretcher attachments before asking Ron to take off. We flew down and landed by the others on the shelf. I unclipped Mark and then returned up to Porter Col. This time I clipped Phil on to the strop directly by his harness. We were only on the ground fifteen to twenty seconds. As we landed by the others the cloud was starting to

179

spill over the top of the mountain from the Tasman Glacier and around the West Ridge.

A last word from the joint proprietor of Middle Peak Hotel, now closed for the season:

Finally – slumped in the front passenger seat of HWW. They didn't let me walk; no one realising the damage was already done, long before. Fumbling again with the belt fastener, just like the last time. Chewing on Dick's liquorice, staring alternately at the instrument panel and Ron – talking to his headset – wondering what he is saying. Bill's out there somewhere, flying back-up in HMV. I remember Don told me that, coming down on the strop.

Snug, isolated in the machine, away from the mountain and the cold, watching the dials. A glance out through the windscreen. A jolt back to reality! Where are we going? Above Haast Ridge, spiralling down towards the Tasman Glacier, to find a way home under the wall of snow clouds. Stunned – realising then the incredible commitment these guys have made – my tears roll freely as Dick leans over with more liquorice. His grinning nod says Mark is OK too.

POSTSCRIPT

A month later on Christmas Eve both climbers had their frostbitten feet amputated. Five months later after learning to walk on their artificial legs, Mark Inglis was back at work at Mount Cook National Park Headquarters and Phil Doole left with a climbing team on an expedition to the Peruvian Andes. Ron Small was awarded the MBE for his part in this and many other rescues. Ken Joyce was later killed in a plane crash on the Tasman Glacier.

10

SHIBBOLETH

I suppose if you take any given area of the earth's crust, it will have its tale to tell. What secrets does a square yard of battlefield hold or the floor of a prison cell? To mountaineers and rescuers certain climbs and peaks present obvious hazards and can be poignant with memories. The Eiger North Wall, for example, is notorious for stone fall and storms, the Everest Icefall for tottering séracs and abysmal crevasses, and Mount Washington for high winds. Each rescue team has its local accident black spots into which team members would never dream of venturing in bad conditions of their own accord. A call-out removes the option.

Buachaille Etive Mor in Glencoe is a peak which seems to stand as self-appointed guardian over the Moor of Rannoch. By international standards it is not a big mountain; but like many smaller peaks it reaps its macabre harvest as assiduously as its big brothers: probably more climbers have been killed on this conical lump of porphyry than on the Eiger itself.

Great Gully of the Buachaille is a steep-sided wound which appears to have been gouged out by an almighty bulldozer and left unhealed for those wishing to inspect the innards of the mountain. In summer it spews forth rocks at irregular intervals and in the winter, avalanches. From its sombre depths we rescue unfortunate climbers every year. In summer the gully does not present a rock climb as such, though it possibly has a soggy attraction for athletic botanists. (Winter is another matter entirely.) But in summer the walls on either side of the gully present sport of a vertical and intimidating nature, especially the great sweep of rock on the left, known for obvious reasons as Slime Wall. To its right, with the symmetrical uniformity of a dank tenement close but superbly executed, is the slit of Raven's Gully. To the right again, separated by a buttress, is Great Gully. Raven's Gully and Slime Wall both present a challenge to mountaineers. The uncompromising steepness of Slime Wall provides a playground for those to whom movement on rock is an art form. In winter Raven's Gully presents high-angled overhanging sport to climbers who dare enter between its claustrophobic walls.

In winter too Great Gully is the climbing M1 of the Buachaille and appears to induce motorway madness in climbers attracted to it when it is obviously poised with unconsolidated snow and hopelessly out of condition.

This tale takes place in 1958, the venue Slime Wall, the route Shibboleth. The climbers were Andrew Fraser (now an Edinburgh GP) and Robin Smith. I knew Robin well. He was possibly the most promising climber of his generation, a man of apparently unlimited strength, with an analytical mind. In a few years he had created a new dimension in mountaineering, raising the standard in both winter and summer. Sadly, he was to fall to his death four years later on a descent in the Pamirs with Wilfred Noyce. One slipped (an eye-witness is not sure which one) and pulled the other off. Though the first person to fall managed to stop he couldn't then hold his companion on the rope and so both plunged to their deaths. I remember Robin awakening on my floor in Glencoe where he used to doss from time to time, covered in feathers which had moulted overnight from his ancient sleeping bag. The down clung to his hairy cardigan, a legacy from his grand-mother, and there it remained until the west-coast winds plucked it off and he again took on a human aspect rather than a cross between an eider duck chick and an orang-outang. As Andrew Fraser, author of the following account recalls, Robin is the hero of Slime Wall.

ANDREW FRASER

My account of the climb is taken from the *Edinburgh University Mountaineering Club Journal* of 1959. It is a period piece, written with student enthusiasm, but it may recapture something of the flavour of climbing with Robin Smith in those days when he was establishing himself as one of the finest climbers of the time.

A few paragraphs will help to set the scene. Robin was a student at the University of Edinburgh, but his philosophy course left him plenty of time for climbing, the dominant obsession of his life. During these years the EUMC gave him a good supply of enthusiastic seconds; I had an easy term, a tent and the occasional use of a vehicle and was quickly drawn into the summer's schemes. The forthcoming new edition of the Scottish Mountaineering Club *Glencoe Rock-Climbing Guide* was a great incentive to polish off the best remaining lines on the Buachaille before the editor's deadline, and most weekends found us in the cluster of scruffy little tents at Gunpowder Green at the base of the mountain. The rival camp usually arrived in Graham Tiso's old Ford Popular – Big Ellie, Dougal Haston, Ronnie Marshall and the legendary Old Man Marshall himself, one of Scotland's great climbers.

Jimmy Marshall dominated our activities, subtly stirring up the competitive spirit amongst the young tigers, pitting Robin against the Currie Boys (an outrider of Edinburgh, where Dougal Haston came from), and hard men against soft students; Edinburgh youth against Creagh Dhu classics. Rivalry bred gamesmanship. Plans were kept secret. Robin would mutter vaguely about strolling up to have a look at one of the golden oldie routes, if he felt up to it; Dougal and Ellie would talk of maybe getting into training on a V. Diff or two; Jimmy would apparently prepare to sleep quietly in the sun at the camp site. But each nursed his own schemes. Despite a leisurely start, the casual walk up the hill would turn into a race for the cliffs, with Big Ellie's ribald roars chasing us up Great Gully, and always the possibility that Jimmy Marshall would materialise by magic at the foot of the great new line before we reached it, even though we had left him still in his sleeping bag at the camp. Insults and taunts flew between the cliffs. Standards rose. The Buachaille was cleaned up, and the focus could move further down Glencoe for next season.

Robin's writing was as influential as his climbing, and his articles for the *Edinburgh University Mountaineering Club Journal* have become classics. His own tale of Shibboleth would have been very different. When I wrote this account of our climb we spent many hours in the little café in Forrest Road, Edinburgh, where so many of our plans were concocted, going over the details with my crutches propped against the wall.

Shibboleth

This is the story of Shibboleth – the true story behind the sensational headlines in the *Daily Record* of Monday 16 June 1958. SEVEN INCHES FROM DEATH shouted the inch-high block letters; 'Hurt Youth Saved on Mountain' ran the sub-heading . . .

But, to begin at the beginning. The principal characters in the tale are a certain Robin Smith and a cliff on the Buachaille Etive Mor, promisingly known as Slime Wall. Early in the summer Robin set his mind on forcing a Great New Route straight up the virgin verticality of this fearsome face, but up till June the weather kept him grounded. He passed his time thinking up a worthy name for his adversary, eventually, for reasons known only to himself and certain of the Gileadites, to fix on Shibboleth. He pondered long on the choice and was often to be seen in some small café of the town with a visionary gleam in his eye, muttering the word to himself, weighing it up, savouring its quality, testing its quantities, passing slowly from initial soft sibilant syllable to linger long on limpid labial and liquid 'l', endowing the word in a rapture of phonetic sensuality with almost oracular portent.

When at last summer arrived and the slime had drawn sulkily back into streaky patches, Robin decided to renew the attack. He lacked only a sufficiently docile second to hold the other end of his rope so, with glowing tales of a Great Natural Line, he lured me off to Glencoe. When he had tied me securely to the first belay and I had time to study the projected route, all I could make out of his Great Natural Line was a series of highly unnatural cracks and corners extending tenuously up the 500 feet of sheer rock above me, linked, or rather separated by, sections of steep smooth slab. This is one of those spots which drive home the meaning of 'vertical, if not overhanging' – a phrase which was to be much used on the ascent.

This is not the place for a detailed technical description, but a vague sketch may prove of use. The climb is 550 feet long and consists of six pitches, each of which is of very severe grading, then the highest standard. The first pitch is shared with a climb called Guerdon Grooves and merely serves as mild preparatory exercise. Pitch 2 is the hardest and never falls below VS over all its 90 feet while pitches 3 and 4 are nearly as hard. The last two pitches are more straightforward again and are even separated by a platform big enough to stand on without using the hands, though the exposure discourages this somewhat. At the hard bits a harsh croak emanates from Raven's Gully, while at the desperate bits I had the distinct impression of vultures hovering behind me, though this may have been merely imagination.

We spent two weekends on the climb. The first day we climbed the lower three pitches. Robin spent a considerable time clinging to the face below the crux, trying vainly to stem the oozing slime with a towel borrowed from an unwitting friend some months before. He abandoned this eventually in favour of simple levitation, and we made fine progress till he was turned back by approaching dusk and the severity of the resistance on pitch 4. We escaped from the face by following the magnificent flake of Revelation, which runs up beside this pitch, but further to the left.

Next day we returned by the start of Revelation to our turning point of the day before. Robin contemplated the fourth pitch anew. The sun was shining all around, accentuating the perpetual damp depressing gloom of Slime Wall. Shibboleth was exerting all her subtle insidious powers of dissuasion. No doubt malnutrition and camp life had left their mark on us too. Anyway, the more we contemplated the situation, the more obvious it became that the ideal way led up the flake pitch of Revelation to the left. From its top one could resume the original line with ease. Robin swore it would be more aesthetic to include such a unique pitch in such a fine climb, while I pointed out that it was in fact the more direct line. And so, up the flake we swarmed, revelling in its beauty and exposure, leaning out carefree on huge undercut holds over a sheer drop into Great Gully some three hundred feet below. At the end of the day we emerged on to the hillside above, with the rest of our climb safely behind us.

It was then that a chill breeze of doubt first struck us, and faint echoes of mocking laughter wafted up out of Raven's Gully. Shibboleth obviously considered that by the inviolate middle pitch she retained her virtue. We could feel her exulting in her subtle triumph. Reluctantly, we climbed down by a fearful loose chimney of Cuneiform Buttress opposite to review the situation. There was no doubt about the direct line.

And so we returned next weekend, vowing to prove for once and for all who was master. An alpine start from base camp saw us at the foot of the climb by midday. The second pitch provided some entertainment when it came to my turn to follow Robin's graceful lead. At the crux he had fixed a piton. This was the only one used in the whole climb apart from belays and was essential for security, the nearest runner being thirty feet below and the next hold being fifteen feet above, up a smooth overhanging corner. Since the piton filled the vital handhold before the crux, I at least was very glad to use it quite unscrupulously. But being second, I had to remove it as I passed. The only position in which I could hold on with one hand and hammer with the other was so low as to be prohibitively exhausting. So I had to pull up to the piton and lean fully out from it with my left hand and hammer with my right while Robin took my weight on the rope from above. There was only a trace of a hold for my left foot while my right just pushed flat against the gently overhanging wall stretching massively on my right down to the last belay.

I hammered till I was exhausted; the peg wiggled freely, but was firmly pinched about its middle. At last I got permission from Robin to leave it behind. Just before continuing up I gave it a couple of desultory blows as a final gesture – and found myself floating gracefully away out from the climb and in again to the impossible wall on my right, clutching the recalcitrant peg in my hand. Great gusts of drain-like laughter echoed down to me. All I could do was push off gently again and hope to arrive back where I had come from. Somehow I managed to wedge a fingertip in the empty piton crack and hold myself into the cliff, but once there the situation called for urgent action.

I was exhausted. I could not rest from the piton now. I could not climb on, deprived of the piton. I could not face the thought of being lowered right down and starting again – without the piton. The only solution was an inelegant but quick and effective technique specially devised for following Robin on such occasions. It involves liberal use of rope handholds, a jerky and positive 'tight-rope' policy and unscrupulous use of such minimal rugosities as may appear on the actual rock. Any lack of co-ordination tends to leave the second upside down dangling helplessly at the end of the rope, but happily we had perfected the technique on other occasions and all went well.

It is, however, a fairly energetic procedure. When I reached the belay I was utterly shattered and had to cling weakly to the rock for several minutes before I could find sufficient strength to weave myself into the network of loops that constituted the belay, and could let myself relax and recover.

After this somewhat exhausting incident all went well for a while. The virgin fourth pitch was assaulted and duly succumbed to Robin's persuasive tactics. It proved a very worthy pitch and we emerged from it with triumphant feelings – Shibboleth had at last fallen, nothing could take that away from us now. There only remained two pitches. We had agreed beforehand that I should lead the next pitch as a reward for my patience over the many hours we had spent on the limb.

It was the easiest pitch we should encounter, or rather, the least difficult, and I had followed up it quite competently the week before. Robin was belayed to a piton in a reasonable stance, and as I set off he was chortling Shibboleth in a happy way to himself and working out suitably laconic descriptions for the guide book. But Shibboleth is a lady of strong character and she could not take this defeat lightly. She had to be avenged for her fall, and nothing short of human sacrifice could satisfy her outraged pride!

I climbed fifteen feet up and to the right, to the foot of a shallow overhanging corner. This was fifteen feet high and the crux of the pitch, followed by easier rock to the large platform and a fine stance. I remembered that Robin's runner had fallen off as he climbed this corner so I cast around for a better one.

Classic rock spikes are not one of Slime Wall's notable features, but at last I managed to chip out a crack with the hammer so that a single strand of baby nylon would just lie in it. Hoping it was adequate, I clipped one of the ropes into the karabiner and attacked the corner. It was typical of Slime Wall. The main face sloped gently outwards over me, while the shallow right-hand wall remained obligingly vertical. There were a few sideways holds in the crack inside the right-angled corner, and one or two little ledges on the walls but nothing much bigger than fingertip holds.

I was nearly at the top when I realised that my hands were feeling the strain of seven and a half hours' struggling on this cold, damp, steep, sunless wall. My fingers began to feel soft and weak, and showed an alarming tendency to straighten out when I put my full weight on them. But I just had to put my full weight on them for I was in a sort of layback position, my feet pressing in rather than down, since there wasn't enough to press down on, and my body leaning down and out on my arms, since the slope of the wall pushed it that way. My right hand had its fingers curled backhand against a vertical groove on the side wall, while my left hand was pulling sideways against the corner crack and taking most of my weight.

The next move was obvious. There was no choice. I had to lean fully out on my right hand and throw my left hand up on to a ledge above me. This ledge was quite large and flat; it sloped outwards, had a rounded edge and no trace of a grip for the fingers on the inside. I could not lean out on this hold, I could only push down on it as I overtook it. Thus my right hand would have to take my full weight as I moved my foot up to a small ledge at knee level, and gently straightened my leg – leaning right out on my hand. Then my left hand could get a push hold on the ledge while I threw my right up on to large holds and could climb out of the corner to safety.

The more I thought about it, the less likely it seemed that my fingers could hold out. Yet the longer I waited the more tired they became. I couldn't possibly rest them in this position and it was even more strenuous to retreat. To have shouted to Robin would have meant psychological defeat – my fingers would have loosened at once. I knew he was watching me in any case – he had even stopped singing his usual appalling skiffle. I just had to try that move.

I summoned up my last reserves of energy and leaned right out. I put my hand up on the ledge and moved my foot up. But I felt my hand weakening as I tried to straighten my leg and swing up gently, and then my fingers turned to putty. I seemed to be watching impersonally as I saw them straighten out and leave the rock. I started to fall. Classically my whole life should have flashed before me but my mind remained a rather peaceful blank; it was almost a feeling of relief – I had done my best and it was out of my hands now.

The next thing I knew was a hefty jerk at my waist which doubled me up, and I found myself dangling at the end of the rope some thirty feet down at a level with Robin, but over to the right. I contemplated cursing roundly but decided it was a little melodramatic. The runner which I had spent so long making had stayed put. The rope had not broken. Robin had held me. His piton hadn't come out. Everything seemed to have gone off classically until I became aware of a burning heat in my right leg. A quick glance down led to an instant diagnosis of broken; my foot was swinging about quite regardless of what I did with my leg. It must have hit the ledge where the runner was, for it was so steep elsewhere that I had fallen quite free of the rock and wasn't even bruised or scratched otherwise.

But the fates had kindly provided a nice ledge a couple of feet below. Robin lowered me to it. It was about a foot wide and eighteen inches long, and was quite unique on the face – there was nothing comparable in sight. I managed to sit on it dangling my leg over the edge. Robin passed over his end of the rope and I tied it to my waistline so that I was really suspended on to the ledge from the runner and couldn't fall off if I fainted. I had the rock behind me and to my right and the two ends of the rope like braces in front of me. I was as comfortable as I could hope to be, though a little cramped, and all I had to do was to prevent my foot swinging about.

We shouted for help, but our cries were swallowed up in the echoes of Great Gully. So Robin tied the end of his rope to the piton and traversed off more or less unprotected over some sixty feet of far from easy rock at a considerable exposure.

From my ledge one could have spat, if one were that kind of person, straight to the bottom of Great Gully, 300 feet below.

I looked at my watch – 7.30. Then I set about examining my leg. Both bones were obviously broken clean through about halfway up the shin; I could feel the ends grinding together on the slightest provocation. As long as I kept perfectly still it only felt hot, but any movement was distinctly painful. All the rules told me I should develop shock, but my pulse obstinately refused to rise over the 100 level. Then I wondered how I was going to be got off; there was 300 sheer feet below me and 200 feet above. As I couldn't solve that one I tried not to think of the immediate future. How long did a leg take to heal? Six weeks, I seemed to remember. I hate to think what I should have felt if I had known it would take six months! Then my foot began to feel numb and cold, so I loosened the lace of my boot very gently.

It seemed quite soon, though it was actually two hours later, when I heard Robin's voice from the top of the cliff again. The rescue party was on its way. He climbed over to me and kept me cheerful till the experts arrived to plan the operation from the far side of Great Gully. Apparently people had never fallen off in such an interesting place before, or at least they hadn't survived to be rescued. Splints were lowered and we fixed them fairly efficiently. The stretcher was manhandled up Great Gully beneath us with much gentle cursing. The air was ringing with Glasgow and Edinburgh voices and the hillside seemed to be alive with climbers.

Ropes were lowered to us from above, knotted to reach down the 200 feet. I tied myself into a cradle arrangement, leaving my legs dangling. Then Robin tied another rope on to me – I don't think he trusted my knots – and tied himself on to a third. I tied my feet together to give me some control of my right foot. Two more ropes were brought over from the side of the cliff, where there was a largish platform on North Buttress, and we tied on to them too. Then we let the top ropes take our weight, while we were pulled over and up to the platform. Robin was half-pulled and half-climbed across the face, protecting me and controlling the ropes, while I rested on his arms and fended off with my hands. It was quite a feat getting five long stretchy ropes to work in perfect co-ordination.

Five hours after my fall I was off the cliff and safely on the platform. I could lie down at last and stretch myself again. A unique hot drink consisting mainly of chocolate had been brewed on the hillside, thanks to Graham Tiso who worked for Cadbury's. Then I was carefully inserted into a Thomas splint, wrapped in a sleeping bag and blankets and strapped securely into the stretcher. Familiar and unfamiliar faces floated into my sight and away again – I didn't gather who half the people were, but they seemed to be a good mixture of Scottish climbing clubs.

Now the real work started. Happily I had chosen a fine clear midsummer's night, but even so the North Buttress is no place to take a stretcher down at midnight. So the route lay upwards. The technique was magnificent: five ropes were tied to the head of the stretcher and teams of seemingly inexhaustible climbers simply pulled me up the buttress. A Glasgow man was in the straps at the foot of the stretcher and he was pulled up too. He just had to walk up the face steadying the stretcher in a sort of inverted abseil. On the less steep bits indefatigable relays of climbers manhandled me up the hillside, half sliding me on the ski runners. It was a strange sensation to be relaxed and comfortable, vertically ascending the Buachaille at midnight, with the whole of the Moor of Rannoch, the Kingshouse, the camp site and the Etive laid out flat at my feet in the midsummer dusk.

I was hauled up the hill for some time, then over long scree traverses under grey cliffs, the rescuers slithering and scrabbling round the mountain until we could make our way down Lagangarbh Gully and over the moor to the road. I didn't quite keep track of the whole journey, nor could I contribute much to the general flow of conversation of the party; the stretcher was so comfortable and so smoothly carried that I felt more inclined to go to sleep.

The rescue party was magnificent. A better, more experienced group of climbers it would be hard to assemble in Scotland; most of the best-known characters in active Scottish climbing were there. They had been dragged from their tents or the Kingshouse back on to the hill for an exhausting all-night expedition, many without their suppers, but the tone of the party was amazing. I would never have imagined that a rescue could be so cheerful; everyone seemed to regard it as the most entertaining expedition of the season. There was a lot of good-natured inter-city banter and abuse; I gathered that one Glasgow fellow seemed to think that Edinburgh had been trespassing on *his* wall, and that my fall was the just and awful retribution of the gods. Another had the distinct impression that this was a god-sent exclusive scoop for his newspaper and promised me headlines next day. We all joined in with suggestions that would really impress the great British public, but I have to confess the actual result was even more sensational.

We reached the roadside as dawn was breaking and everyone lay around exhausted, wondering whether to eat or to sleep first. Eventually they divided the day fairly evenly between the two; happily the weather wasn't of the sort to tempt them on to the hill again. A Bedford van took me to Fort William. When we met the ambulance after a mile or two the owner of the van just persuaded it to go home again empty and very kindly took me all the way. And so, just twelve hours after I had fallen in the most inaccessible spot on the Buachaille, I reached the Belford Hospital and the friendly capable hands of Dr Duff and his charming staff.